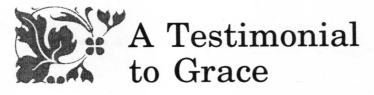

A Testimonial to Grace

and

Reflections on a Theological Journey

Avery Dulles, S.J.

50th Anniversary Edition

Sheed & Ward
Kansas City

Sheed & Ward™ is a service of The National Catholic Reporter Publishing Company.

Library of Congress Cataloging-in-Publication Data
    Dulles, Avery Robert, 1918-
    A testimonial to grace and reflections on a theological journey / Avery Dulles. — 50th anniversary ed.
        p.   cm.
    Includes: A testimonial to grace.
    Includes bibliographical references.
    ISBN: 1-55612-904-1 (alk. paper)
    1. Dulles, Avery Robert, 1918- . 2. Jesuits—United States—Biography. 3. Catholic Church—United States—Clergy—Biography. 4. Spiritual biography—United States. 5. Catholic converts—United States—Biography. 6. Theologians—United States—Biography. 7. Catholic Church—Doctrines—History—20th century. I. Dulles, Avery Robert, 1918- Testimonial to grace. 1996. II. Title.
    BX4705.D867A3   1996
    230'.2'092—dc20
    [B]   96-17941
                                              CIP

Published by: Sheed & Ward
             115 E. Armour Blvd.
             P.O. Box 419492
             Kansas City, MO 64141-6492

To order, call: (800) 333-7373

Contents

Foreword
to the First Edition

I have often been asked why I became a Catholic. The only sufficient cause for any conversion is, of course, divine grace, for which man can give no explanation. But since grace normally operates by supplying impetus to the will and light to the mind, the question can be answered, on the natural plane, by rendering an account of one's personal motivations. This I was never able to do at all adequately until, thanks to a period of relative leisure at sea during World War II, I had an opportunity to reflect somewhat carefully on the processes by which my ideas had evolved. At that time I set down the reminiscences here published.

The narrative falls, chronologically, into two sections, devoted respectively to the search for sound philosophic values and to the scrutiny of religious doctrines. The formation of my views on these matters will, I trust, be of interest to others who are not unwilling to face those fundamental philosophic and religious problems which have ever been the chief concern of the wise. For it is a task of theirs, as it has been of mine, to establish their own position in relation to those systems of thought – such as skepticism, materialism, and liberalism – which, as I have tried to indicate, hold almost unchallenged sway in our secular universities and thus set the tenor of our intellectual life.

May 20, 1946
Cambridge, Mass.

Foreword
to the 1996 Edition

I composed *A Testimonial to Grace* aboard the cruiser *Philadelphia* in the early fall of 1944. Having just completed an assigment as a liaison officer with the French navy, I was kept waiting for several weeks before receiving official orders to join the staff of the Commander of the Eighth Fleet, which then consisted of the United States Naval Forces in the Mediterranean. To escape the boredom of involuntary idleness, I turned to the typewriter. For some time I had wanted to have a record, if only for myself, of the mental processes that had led me to join the Catholic Church in the fall of 1940, as a first-year law student at Harvard.

First published in 1946, the book went through a number of printings in the next decade. In recent years I have received many requests to reissue and update the story. In 1995 Robert Heyer, as editor-in-chief of the new Sheed & Ward, proposed to me that, since the original bore a Sheed & Ward imprint, his firm might appropriately issue a jubilee edition.

To republish the book after so many years was not unproblematical. I had written it as a young layman, before undertaking a formal study of theology. In composing it, I lacked access to a

library for checking points of information. And
the religious world differed vastly from that of
the late twentieth century. Catholic biblical studies were still at an early stage; the ecumenical
movement had hardly been launched; and the
vast changes introduced by the Second Vatican
Council were still undreamt of.

Nevertheless, the past remains what it was.
My voyage of discovery could not be altered in
retrospect. There could be no question of rewrit-
ing the book over again fifty years later, when
my memories of those early years had become
less vivid. Recognizing some flaws in the biblical
exegesis and factual details, I have added several
new footnotes, which are placed in brackets to
distinguish them from footnotes belonging to the
orginal text. Also, at the publisher's suggestion,
I have assigned titles to the two chapters of the
original book. Otherwise, I reissue the work in
unaltered form, even as regards matters of style,
orthography, and punctuation, so as to keep the
atmosphere of the original. While some of these
matters would have to be changed if I were re-
writing the book today, I am convinced that its
central message is as valid and necessary today
as when I first expressed it.

Robert Heyer suggested that I might add a
chapter on my theological journey over the past
fifty years. Having been a close observer of the
Second Vatican Council and the post-Conciliar
ferment, I gladly acceded to this request. It has
been my privilege to devote much of my lifetime

to a further exploration of the themes (such as revelation, faith, apologetics, and ecclesiology) that first captured my enthusiam as a college undergraduate. In surveying my theological pilgrimage I have tried to bring out the continuity within change that is so much a part of the history of the Church as well as of my own pilgrimage. The glow of evening, I have found, resembles that of early morning — no doubt, because the sun itself remains the same.

July 31, 1996
New York, NY

For
WILLIAM F. MACOMBER
Fellow-wayfarer

A Testimonial to Grace

1. The Human Search

The Human Search

I entered Harvard College in the fall of 1936, having been trained in one of the "better" nonsectarian boarding schools of New England. At that time I possessed, like most of my comrades, a fairly complete but equally naïve philosophy of life, founded on a variety of popular superstitions of a type all too often infused into adolescent minds by well-meaning teachers of physics, history, and literature.

In the first place, I considered it a proved fact that the original and uncreated reality, the sufficient cause of the whole universe, was physical matter, presumably in the form of irreducible atoms or ever circling electronic particles. Following the laws of its own nature, this primeval matter had apparently, at some unspecified period in the remote past, congregated into certain large globular masses. From one such mass, that whirling ball of fire called the sun, our earth had chanced to be cast off, and on our cooling planet, by a further accident, life had emerged. Eventually, through an indefinitely repeated process of variation and natural selection, life had, it seemed, evolved into its human form.

It did not enter my mind to consider that the world owed its existence to a wise Creator, that a beneficent Providence watched over and directed it, or that the soul, as the loving work of God's hands, possessed an eternal destiny. When I contemplated death, as I not infrequently did, I was never troubled by Hamlet's fear of finding there anything different from the peace of oblivion. I took it for granted that the human spirit was completely dependent for its existence and operation on the life of the body. The workings of the spirit, including the processes of thought itself, I considered to be a pale reflection of interrelated physical activities in the brain.

The religious and moral aspects of such a cosmology are only too obvious. Manifestly, there was in it no room for God. Every notion of God was in my opinion a sort of *deus ex machina,* an invention of the human mind to explain away facts which could not be otherwise accounted for. Just as scientific progress had, as I imagined, made it unnecessary to assume that God periodically intervened in the universe, so too, I inferred, it was gradually becoming superfluous to posit a supernatural First Winder of the universal clock.

Man having been produced by chance, it seemed illusory to hold that he had any ordained end or was subject to any moral strictures not of his own making. Morality, then, could be interpreted as a texture of conventions woven by the ingenuity of men for reasons of convenience. "Revealed" religion I dismissed as a vain attempt to find sanctions (where none in truth existed) for such conduct and mental attitudes as proved conducive to social well-being.

I regarded it as a rather unfortunate fact that, in view of the progress of science – and especially, for some obscure reason, the discovery of evolution – intelligent men could no longer believe in the immortality of the human soul. As a result, I judged, supernatural religion was now relegated to the realm of superstition, and morality exposed in its true guise, as a sort of social contract expressive of the general desires of the community. No longer did there exist any power which could be invoked to deter the contracting parties from cheating a little to their own advantage – other than the risk of being caught and penalized by their fellow men. And, in view of the lawlessness of the universe, I could feel little indignation against those who violated a few clauses of the ethical code.

Though not personally a great cheater at the game of life, I adhered to my own premises logically enough to be frankly out for myself alone. I considered it a platitude that everyone, by an irresistible law of his being, sought only his own personal satisfaction, and that "unselfishness" must consequently be regarded as either hypocrisy or insanity. A moderate respect for the aspirations of others was, however, a necessary concomitant of enlightened self-interest.

The "happiness" which was the universal object of human endeavor might, in my judgment, be sought under any of a number of forms. Some, to be sure, bent their efforts to obtaining merely the grosser forms of pleasure, but for my part, while I did not condemn these others, I never identified happiness exclusively with ease or sensual delight. The romantic element was strong enough in my nature to persuade me that there existed a deeper kind of happiness, from which struggle was never absent. The eternal servitude of Prometheus, whom naught could compel to yield to the gods, seemed to me to represent a more valid conception of heaven than did the eternal bliss of the angels. To partake fully of life was, I believed, to strive unceasingly like Goethe's Faust. To be content, on the other hand, was in a sense to die.

The Promethean heritage, the fire of the gods, seemed to be immortalized in the arts; and I was greatly devoted to painting and poetry, though I had no ear for music. Art I revered as the expression of the divine element, the everlasting prize of joy in conflict, by the acquisition of which man rises above himself. In art I found preserved and canonized the deepest and most sublime experience of man, and depth of personal experience was for me identical with human excellence. Success in life, I held with Walter Pater, was to burn always with a "hard, gemlike flame."

This rapturous delight, this elixir of life, had nothing in common with savage fury or animal contentment. The passions of the many were lacking in glamour, elegance, and subtlety. For the desires and tenets of the vast majority I felt an indifference coupled with a touch of Ibsen's contempt.[1] The rarefied excellence which I esteemed was passion distilled by the white heat of its own intensity and crystallized in lasting form by creative achievement on the intellectual plane. This chemical refinement of emotion was, I noted, most perfectly effected in the isolation of the proverbial ivory tower. The tranquil ecstasy of the "escapists" aroused my admiration and enthusiasm. My favorite painter was the retiring Cézanne. Arthur Rimbaud and Wallace Stevens had achieved in verse the esoteric quality which I admired.

My political ideas, if I can be said to have had ideas on a subject which I regarded as insufferably prosaic, were summed up in a solemn dislike for regimentation. The rapid advance of collectivized production was hateful to me because it threatened to engender a society which supplied neither stimulus nor outlet for artistic energies. The anesthetizing routine of the average life, which dulled the artistic sensibilities and inhibited the creative ferment in the individual spirit, was the epitome of all that I rebelled against. The notion of discipline from any quarter – and above all from the ineluctable power of the State – aroused my resentment. My Utopia was a society which gave to each the freedom to seek his own brand of happiness, and to the elite the opportunity of stealing fire from the gods. The best government, I would recite, is that which

---

1. As expressed, for example, in *An Enemy of the People.*

governs least. Mill's *Essay on Liberty* was my
political *Credo.*

My first year in college did little to upset the
scheme of values which I had formulated and
espoused while in preparatory school. During this
year I studied no philosophy course, and from the
courses in history and literature which I attended
I imbibed only the positivism of Auguste Comte,
which served to entrench me further in materialism. I felt a vague sympathy for every social
movement styled as "liberal," and read with un-
critical veneration the political manifestos of such
diverse authors as Thomas Mann, André Mal-
raux, and Ernest Hemingway.

Desisting somewhat from artistic pursuits, I
took up at this time the cult of what is called
"experience." As a result, my freshman year was
a wild and chaotic year, marked by an excess of
drinking and a corresponding deficiency of sleep.
My room, distinguished by the possession of a
percolator, became a center of nocturnal revelry.
Whole nights were passed in aimless jocularity
either here or in shoddy Boston bars. My attendance at classes was casual at best.

This manner of life was abruptly altered in
April, at which time two of my closest friends
were expelled from college as the result of a mid-
night adventure in which the Boston police saw
fit to intervene. I myself narrowly escaped expul-
sion for complicity in the same offense: the University's Administrative Board having reached a
favorable decision in my case thanks to the swing-

ing of a single vote in the third ballot of their deliberations. After that incident I settled down a little, chastened perhaps by the narrowness of this escape, but also convinced by trial and error that I could derive little satisfaction from engaging in disorderly escapades.

My nearest friend, after my two less fortunate comrades had been dismissed, was not a university student but a waiter on the night shift in a Cambridge cafeteria which was one of my customary nocturnal haunts. Frank Stacy was a Cambridge lad about my own age. His background was one of poverty and squalor, but, endowed with a fine and ever active mind, he had read widely, and combined in his person the gifts of a keen intelligence and a thoroughly engaging manner. He and I would meet regularly about three o'clock in the morning, at which time he got off from work, and pass the hours from then until the beginning of my morning classes discussing eagerly the works of Dylan Thomas, James Joyce, and other contemporary writers of poetry and fiction. Born and bred a Catholic, Stacy had lost his faith, and I certainly did little to restore it to him. I remember being genuinely amazed when in an unguarded moment he ventured the opinion that man, being possessed of reason, was specifically different from the other animals – a little suggestion which the good sisters had left with him in his childhood. Every educated person, I had imagined, understood that there was no qualitative distinction between the human and simian mind, but a distinction only of degree.

Another of my intimate friends, named Edwin Selden, belonged to a small clique of freshmen who gathered themselves about an Anglo-Catholic priest widely known under the title of Father Smythe. Besides being very devout, this coterie were ardent supporters of every Communist measure and rally, which struck me then, and still strikes me, as strangely inconsistent. I never joined them at their "Mass" or devotions, but I did once accept an invitation to go over for tea with Father Smythe. A rather handsome man in his middle forties, he impressed me, as he sat in his room of antique English furnishings, as both learned and likeable. The conversation, perhaps because of my presence, was rather matter of fact: and I confess that I was little interested in being proselytized. Selden, wiser in this respect than I, was unable to understand my indifference. I remember him asking me one time, after I had expressed complete satisfaction with being an atheist, "But haven't you any religious *feeling?*" I am afraid that I had none, nor did I care to have, because I was convinced that I could never found my faith on feeling.

Selden startled me further on another occasion by confiding to me in a whispered tone: "We hope to go over to Rome someday." Amazed, I was powerless to ask him how, if he believed in the divine authority of the Pope, he could dare to delay, and how, if he disbelieved, he could aspire to make this transfer of allegiance. Perhaps he and his companions were amassing their forces so that when they came into the Church they could drive a good bargain such as, for example, the repeal of the dogma of the Immaculate Conception. In any case, I am sure that they would have found my thinking on such matters too simple. I have quite lost track of Selden, for he left college at the end of my freshman year. I hope that he has gotten over to Rome, God bless him.

My second year in college was intellectually more fruitful than the first. My life at this point assumed a stabler and more sedentary form. I took a general course in philosophy which, introducing me to the works of Aristotle and Plato, made me perceive how much sounder was their outlook on the universe than the narrow mathematicism of Descartes and Spinoza or the sterile skepticism of Hume and Kant. The modern philosophers seemed to stultify themselves by erecting enormous epistemological difficulties at the outset. The Greeks, on the other hand, without neglecting the problem of knowledge, got much further in solving the problem of being.

From Aristotle, whom I studied more intensively in the following year, I acquired a new and far deeper concept of reality. His reasoning forced me to recognize that things are something more than hard atoms or bouncing electrons; that their natures consist less in their underlying matter than in the forms in which that matter is clothed and in the ends to which they are adapted. Matter as such, I came to understand, is passive; it can have no sensible existence and can effect nothing whatever unless it be formed, or patterned, in a certain way. In the light of this discovery I could see plainly the absurdity of declaring that the most real stage of existence was on the plane of minimum organization. On the contrary, the most highly organized being was the most active and the most real. Simple electronic vibrations were but one step removed from total non-existence.

Once I had admitted the concept of degrees of reality, ranging from the most indeterminate to the most fully actuated, I was capable of distinguishing between that which is "real" and that which is "material." Matter, because it could be molded into various shapes, became associated in my thought with the potential; form, because it was the determining principle, with the actual. I could then understand how the Supreme Being, as "Pure Act," impassible and immutable, might be altogether immaterial, and how the spiritual soul, as the "informing" principle in man, might be capable of subsisting apart from its material partner, the body.

From Aristotle, too, I learned to respect final causes. It was a tremendous step forward when I first became aware that an egg, for example, could not be completely understood by a study of its chemical composition, but that one must take account of the ideal of "chickenness" which it tended to fulfill in order to see both why the egg was constituted as it was and what it was likely to become. Thereafter I had a new notion of the meaning of philosophical explanation. If I wished to understand why a man could see, for example, I was no longer content with a reply which merely described the retina. I demanded to be informed of the purpose of sight. Ultimately the notion of purpose, or design, in my philosophy was to have its fruition in the Christian concept of Providence; but that development comes later in this narrative.

The most important influence of Aristotle on my philosophic outlook was that he gave me a totally new conception of the relation between thought and the extra-mental world. Before reading Aristotle I had been haunted by the impression that the mind's perceptions were insuperably subjective and distorted, and that extra-mental reality was something hard, unfriendly, and impenetrable. When one designated an object as round, or flat, or whatever, I considered that this was a convenient but rather careless way of describing a mental reaction, which might be a very inaccurate representation of the *Ding an sich*. At best, the predicates of roundness and flatness seemed to be tenuous hypotheses about objective realities, likely to be upset at any moment by a new discovery of Einstein.

Aristotle convinced me that the outer world was not so unattainable to the senses and the mind. He restored my confidence in the evidence of the senses by demonstrating that they were inherently susceptible of receiving sensible impressions, that their nature was to be not prison bars but windows of the soul. Reason likewise, I learned from Aristotle, was not a quality which served merely to make man a misfit in an irrational universe. It was, on the contrary, the strongest link between the soul and the outer world, being an integral part of the economy of nature and attuned to the natural law which governed the universe. So extreme had been my previous distrust of reason that even the law of contradiction, as expounded by Aristotle, came to me as a startling revelation. It had never occurred to me before that that which could be shown absurd in logic must *ipso facto* be ontologically impossible.

From the vantage point of these discoveries, I appreciated for the first time in its manifold implications the truth that rational distinctions must necessarily correspond to diversities in fact. From this it followed that the ordered universe of philosophical abstraction was not an artificial one. The chaotic world in which I had been living yielded place to the hierarchic universe of Aristotle. Reality appeared to be stratified on the progressive planes of lifeless matter, vegetable growth, then animal and finally human life (of what came higher in the scale I had as yet no definite intimation).

On apprehending the dignity of reason and its true relation to reality I all at once felt at home in the universe. It is impossible for me to exaggerate the sense of joy and freedom which came from this discovery. I soon found myself reading avidly the modern Aristotelians – Catholic authors such as Jacques Maritain and Étienne Gilson – and adhering to the logic of their doctrine with a fervor which I could hardly today recapture.

If Aristotle persuaded me that the abstractions of reason reflected the structure of reality, Plato, whom I studied concurrently, took me one step further. He convinced me that moral values had an objective basis. My previous opinions in the field of ethics had rested on the assumption that to be virtuous was merely to abide by certain conventions, or canons of behavior, representative of the collective desires of the community. Our ideas of justice, I would have said, were nothing more than a reflection of the subjective desires of particular groups of men. The moral law, even if binding, was neither stable nor universal. Its frontiers were forever shifting and uncertain. Other desires, I argued, other morals. The idea of virtue, thus conceived, held little attraction for me. I could see nothing noble or inspiring in making oneself a pliant instrument of the aspirations of others, however glorious society might wish to make subservience appear. An action which was esthetically correct was more appealing to me than one which was morally sound.

In my esthetic theories, on the other hand, I was already half a Platonist. I accepted the existence of objective standards of beauty. I was thoroughly familiar with that specious line of argument which represented the sense of beauty as a mere psychological reaction of the individual when confronted with certain phenomena which in themselves were neither beautiful nor ugly. That you or I – so ran the argument – should be thrilled by certain combinations of noises did not prove that those noises had anything particularly commendable in themselves, or that there was any justification for requiring others to have the same reaction as ourselves. Such esthetic relativism I utterly rejected, refuting its contentions by an analysis of the "creative" process. The artist, I observed, aimed ever to embody in lasting form the ideal which, by a mysterious process, sprang up within his soul. At the moment of his labors he was, commonly enough, rapt in the vision of beauty which he beheld and virtually unconscious of any potential audience. That others later enjoyed and praised his work was proof, not of the artist's intent to entertain, but of the intrinsic merit of his work.

Often, to be sure, great masterpieces had passed unrecognized. That did not, however, detract from their inherent excellence. I could not concede that the artist must cater to the public demand, or that his works should be judged according to their popular acceptance. To arraign them before the fickle court of public acclaim was in effect to set aside the esthetic law and to make a tyrant of the popular taste, which might itself be either good or bad. My own view was that art was governed by a logic of its own (different from the logic of abstract deduction), and that the critic must be schooled in the exacting science of esthetics before he could judge competently about the laws of beauty.

Beauty I considered as something supreme and absolute. Its purpose was fulfilled in its very nature. "A poem," as both Mallarmé and MacLeish had said, "must not mean but be." An ultimate value, beauty was to be sought for itself alone and not for any ulterior end. Self-sufficient, it must not tend toward anything beyond. A poem or play which attempted to inculcate some doctrine or which impelled one to adopt some course of action was, as art, impure. Didacticism was to be accounted a defect. A perfect work of beauty, I maintained, did not even elicit a state of emotion. Beauty was quieting, and its place above laughter and tears. One did not stand weeping in the Louvre, or go home from the *Alcestis* tearing one's hair. The essential note of the vision of beauty was peace, a vibrant peace charged with life and tension, a tranquillity born of the marriage of ecstasy and law.

On becoming acquainted with Plato's Idea of the Good I instantly recognized in it something closely akin to my own intuition of Beauty, transposed to the higher plane of the invisible. If my Beauty was a foretaste of heaven, so too was Plato's Good. Both were self-contained and supreme; each was to be sought for its own sake. Every experience of happiness, said Plato, is to some degree a realization of the Good. A partial attainment, I would have had it, of the beautiful.

Indeed Plato himself explicitly affirmed that the Good and the Beautiful were but one substance taken under different aspects. They were nominally distinct, but really identical, notes of an entity which in itself was unitary and indivisible. With reference to material substances Beauty, Truth and Goodness were but three designations for the same condition – conformity with the ideal pattern laid up in heaven. Beauty, in Plato's philosophy, was not merely that which induced a pleasurable sensation. It was objective excellence, insofar as it elicited acquiescence. That which pleased the senses was but the appearance of beauty. That which thrilled the intellectual vision was beauty itself. Wherever virtue or truth could be found, there beauty was also. Ugliness, conversely, was merely another name for deformity. Nothing untrue to the "forms" of nature could be either beautiful or metaphysically good.

The metaphysical good, for any particular thing, was the most perfect state of its development and internal order. Every action, organ, or object, in Plato's teaching, was to be considered good or evil according to the extent to which it fulfilled the law of its being, or, in his own terms, resembled its eternal Idea. The eye, by this criterion, is good if it sees well, the mind if it thinks well, the seamster if he sews well, the philosopher if he is wise, and the ruler if he is just.

The moral good, in the Platonic system, was that in human action which tended to realize the metaphysical good. For a man to be virtuous, then, he had only to give full scope and development to the various powers of his complex nature, with due observance to their mutual relations of authority and dependence. Preeminence belonged to the faculty of reason, the "eye of the soul," which discerned what was to be sought and what avoided.

The Platonic ideal of virtue had enormous consequences in my personal philosophy. Indeed it supplanted the ideal of sensible beauty as the value which I regarded as ultimate. I had previously, it now seemed, been groping after mere shadows of beauty; the senses had held in my life the position which rightfully belonged to reason. To allow concupiscence, or the desire for human esteem, or any other motive, to cause one to transgress the law governing one's own nature now appeared to me as both unintelligent and immoral. The sovereign faculty of reason alone possessed the vision of ends required for right action. Any course of action which tended to dethrone that faculty or to render the will incapable of mastering the appetites, was, I perceived, intrinsically evil. I therefore determined to spare no effort in introducing order within the inner kingdom of my soul. To succeed in life was, I now considered, to establish reason and justice in joint monarchy in one's personal life. Thus far had I progressed from the dictum of Pater which I have quoted above.

Plato's concept of virtue, unlike my previous notions of morality, was not applicable solely to the interrelations between man and man in society. Its jurisdiction over human action was unlimited and all-embracing. For the metaphysical good, upon which Plato founded his moral system, was identified with every degree and kind of excellence, and therefore coextensive with reality itself. According to Plato, the good was that which all mankind, and indeed the whole of nature, sought but to know, to love, and to imitate. Confronted by the problem of explaining why men, although so motivated, commonly pursued mere shadows rather than the substance of the good, Plato was obliged to posit the existence of some original catastrophe which had darkened the human intellect to the point where mere shadows were mistaken for realities. Thus, by rational inference, he arrived at something analogous to the doctrine of the Fall of Man, although he failed to perceive that (as Revelation teaches) that Fall has left its mark upon the human will as well as upon the intelligence. The function of philosophy, as Plato interpreted it, was but to remove the cloud of darkness which obscured man's vision of the Good. Merely to know perfection, he believed, was already to love it and to seek to realize it in the world.

In addition to being supreme and all-embracing, the Platonic ideal of virtue (which now became my own) was natural, objective and universal. Founded solidly upon the structure of reality, the moral law was to be reckoned not as a mere matter of opinion but as the object of a genuine science. Perceiving that the nature of the good was independent of the flux of human desires, Plato bypassed at once the sterile dichotomies of egoism *versus* altruism and pain *versus* pleasure which are responsible for the futility of so many ethical discussions. The moral law to which he pointed claimed allegiance both in Athens and New York, in the polar regions and in the tropics, whether in the bustle of the marketplace, in the privacy of the home, or in the solitude of a desert island. No matter what one's surroundings, Plato insisted, the qualities proper to man as man remained the same. Wisdom, justice, temperance, and fortitude always and undeniably surpassed their opposites. I was unable to deny that this was so.

In order to complete the foregoing summary of the effect of Plato and Aristotle on my intellectual outlook, I have expounded certain ideas which I did not clearly grasp until the beginning, or even the middle, of my junior year in college, but which began to germinate in my mind when I first studied the writings of these ancient thinkers. Having anticipated certain subsequent developments, I must now ask the reader to return with me to the cold, amoral world in which, philosophically speaking, I still found myself at the beginning of my sophomore year — a world governed only by chance and by the selfish actions of human persons engaged in the cruel quest for pleasure.

The feature which dominates my entire second year at Harvard is that I then made the acquaintance of the man who first gave me a vivid picture of the Catholic faith. His name was Paul Doolin, and he was, through an unmerited dispensation of Providence on my behalf, assigned as my tutor. A convert to the Catholic faith, Doolin was about to leave his teaching position at Harvard to accept an appointment to the faculty of the Jesuit college of Georgetown. But God spared him for me at Harvard long enough so that I was able to study under him for eight months.

A dynamic, black-haired, blue-eyed Irishman, Paul Doolin recaptured in his imagination and reincarnated in his person the spirit of the Middle Ages. Always dramatic, forceful, and sudden in his speech, his technique was to persuade not so much by arguing as by amazing. He could always find a single phrase or observation which went to the absolute root of the matter at hand. He had a marvelous gift for presenting his ideas in concrete terms, without becoming involved in vaporous abstractions, and every word which he spoke was a living expression of his own rich philosophy. His statements were not impartial observations, they were intense personal convictions.

His scheme of values, which seemed a little incongruous in his age and surroundings, was completely at odds with the spirit of the times, at least at Harvard. Doolin was the implacable enemy of materialism, utilitarianism, humanitarianism, pacifism and sentimentality in every form. When asked one time what he would do if given a million dollars, he replied, in his terse, vigorous speech, "Send tanks to Franco." Thus by a single phrase he characteristically opposed himself, not with logic but with his very person, to both the "liberal" interventionists and the pacifist non-interventionists who took sides in nearly every discussion of American foreign policy at the time.

A man cast in the heroic mold, a crusader born out of time, Doolin went to extremes in his denunciation of the prevalent errors. His unsparing mockery extended to sweeping condemnations of whole ages, classes, nations, and races, and occasionally gave rise to misinterpretations. Some considered him an anti-Semite and some a fascist, but both these accusations were unjust.

As a deep Christian, Doolin had an abiding love for all mankind and perhaps specially for the race of Our Lord. His vociferous indignation against the majority of Jews – of whom Marx and Freud were to his mind the aptest symbols – was dogmatic and moral, and ought not to be confused with personal spite or vulgar prejudice.

Doolin's political views were poles apart from fascism. An authoritarian and a legitimist in the

French school, he was on principle, I imagine, an adherent of limited monarchy. He taught a brilliant course in the history of France from the Fifteenth to the Eighteenth Century, the essential thesis of which was to attribute the calamity of the French Revolution to the unscrupulous absolutism of Richelieu and Louis XIV, combined with the bad philosophy of the so-called Enlightenment. A profound student of the history of political thought, Doolin was convinced that that science had died with the age of Jean Bodin and Saint Robert Bellarmine. For modern liberalism he had only the greatest contempt. The Eighteenth Century he dismissed as an "age without political thought," referring to that great constitutional historian, Charles Homer McIlwaine[2], as the author of this perspicacious observation. With his deep sense of the importance of spiritual values, Doolin could not countenance the view of Locke and Montesquieu that the State should concern itself only with the distribution of material things. Like the philosophers of the ancient world, he maintained that the State should take an active part in securing the welfare of souls as well as of bodies. The greatest offense against the State, he would quote from Plato's *Laws,* is to teach error. In Hitler he saw a not untoward revolt against the materialism which had domi-

---

2. [The actual name is Charles Howard McIlwain. I have given it correctly in my reminiscence, "Harvard as an Invitation to Catholicism," in *The Catholics of Harvard Square,* ed. Jeffrey Wills (Petersham, Mass.: St Bede's Publications, 1993), 119-24.]

nated the political thought of the two preceding centuries. Yet he despised most of the canons of National Socialism. The doctrine of the *raison d'état* and the very name of Machiavelli were to him anathema.

Many times I had occasion to discuss with Doolin questions of literature. He had no use, I found, for the seductions of lyric poetry, a form of writing which he characterized, Platonically, as a vain and repulsive display of private sentiment, with special attention to the emotion of self-pity. When I professed a certain admiration for Shakespeare he turned me sharply aside by quoting Milton's criticism:

> . . . sweetest Shakespear fancies childe,
> Warble his native Wood-notes wilde.

To Doolin, Milton's name was magic. More than any other poet, Milton exemplified for him the incomparable superiority of epic over lyric poetry. For all his unsavory connections with the policies of the Protectorate and with Cromwell's dark vengeance on the Irish Catholics, Milton was Doolin's ideal of lofty zeal, integrity, and spiritual grandeur.

> "While the still morn went out with sandals grey. . ."

. . . he would quote reverently, adding with a growl, "That takes imagination!"

The reason behind Doolin's distaste for lyric poetry was fundamentally a moral one. Lyricism, he recognized, was radically sensate and emotional, as opposed to epic or dramatic poetry, which is more commonly what sociologists are wont to label "ideate." Having personally experienced the captivating power of the goddess of beauty, Doolin had formed a deep distrust for the estheticism of the senses. In his Platonic philosophy beauty held a place of honor, provided, however, that it was united with the good. True beauty, in his opinion, must serve to strengthen the moral faculty rather than to stimulate the concupiscent powers of the soul.

To put a label on his philosophy, one might call Doolin a Platonist, or perhaps better an Augustinian. Like the great Carthaginian Bishop of ancient times, Doolin had come to Christianity and to the Catholic Church from a species of Platonism, and particularly from the doctrine of the *Symposium* that love is a force which tends naturally upward toward the divine. Plato, he would say flatly, was very close to Christ.

Doolin's profound grasp and appreciation of the Platonic doctrine of love was, like so many of his intuitions, based on his individual experience. His own approach to Christianity had undoubtedly been wrought through love – as I suspect is the case with all conversions. And love was the great force in Doolin's character which gave him his undeniable power and stature.

Few, however, perceived that this was so. Disdainful of sentimentality, Doolin was methodically reticent and ever at pains to conceal his more tender feelings behind a wall of gruffness. "He doesn't wear his heart on his sleeve," he would say when he wished to compliment someone. The compliment applied admirably to himself. The books which Doolin wrote were so impressive an assemblage of facts and deductions, marshaled with such Euclidian precision, that they read like a lawyer's brief or a treatise on logic. In his lectures, likewise, he studiously avoided all oratory: he would read with lowered chin from little scraps of paper in a monotonous tone of voice. The more superficial students, looking for outward flourish rather than substance, were disappointed or even bored.

I studied under Professor Doolin, as I have said, for only eight months, and was at the time deeply intrenched in the false philosophy which I have described in the first pages of this essay. I was struck principally by the originality of Doolin's opinions. They were a stimulating contrast to all that I had ever heard. Nearly three years were to pass before I found my way into the Catholic Church, but throughout that period the teaching of Paul Doolin was to serve me as a guide and reference point. At the time of hearing it, I was not yet ready to receive Doolin's doctrine, but I treasured it up in the garners of my memory, and drew abundantly therefrom in the years that followed. The reasoning behind some of his sudden and abrupt sentences did not become clear to me until long afterward, but their very obscurity served to make one think, for everything that Doolin said fell into an ultimate pattern. None of his remarks was casual or flippant.

The great importance which Doolin's teaching had for my intellectual development is attributable to the gradual crumbling of my materialist philosophy which began in my sophomore year. I would not have been so receptive to the ideas which I found expressed in the imperishable writings of Plato and Aristotle and in the arresting speech of Paul Doolin except that the inward rottenness of my own philosophy was becoming desperately obvious.

Increasingly I was forced to acknowledge that a life based consistently on the pursuit of pleasure could not be rich either in achievement or in happiness.

An admirer always of the heritage of civilization, I became sadly aware that few of the great achievements of mankind could have been wrought if their authors had been motivated by mere considerations of advantage. The most magnificent works of human architecture were temples and churches, erected for the praise and honor of God. The masterpieces of art which I esteemed were principally religious in character, having as their aim to instruct the faithful, to remind them of their various relationships to God, and to help them to pray rightly to Him and to His saints. When art, in the later Renaissance, became secularized, esthetic delight being made supreme, decadence simultaneously set in. The great voyages of discovery, too, were many of them undertaken with the object of bringing the Christian faith to those who still languished in heathen ignorance. The worldshaking wars of conquest of all ages had been fought, not for the personal satisfaction of the soldiers, but for king, for country and for God.

Often, to be sure, actors had risen to eminence on the stage of life who sought no higher prize than personal wealth or fame or power. But to that extent they had been deluded. They failed to reap the harvest which they sowed, or, like the empire builders who devoted their lives to the amassing of material treasure, they awoke to find themselves grown old and their hoard but dust and ashes in their hands. They would have done better, according to their own standards, to have shortened the arm of their ambition and to have dwelt, like Lucretius or Spinoza, in the peace of a narrow garden.

Indeed my own state of mind was such that I questioned whether they had done well to live at all. The amount of personal pleasure which this world could afford did not seem great enough to compensate for all its loneliness and tears. Private enjoyment was not an adequate guerdon to justify the heartache and the pain. The temptation, therefore, was terribly insistent to extract every drop of pleasure within immediate reach, and then put a term to this dreary existence. I might have done as much except that my thought was developing along new lines.

Love, I perceived, was the strongest impulse of the human heart, yet in my philosophy it held no place. The fatal defect of my outlook in life, oriented as it was toward the pursuit of pleasure, was that it thwarted the most basic human instincts, to love, to labor and to serve. Hence the shallowness and misery of my existence which daily threatened to become intolerable. My philosophy failed me because it was not big enough to contain the human, let alone the heroic. By an odd paradox, I noted, man could find no joy unless he sought it not, unless he lived by love, which "seeketh not her own." Was there, I asked, some other good, above and apart from human enjoyment, capable of eliciting the boundless resources of devotion, loyalty and fortitude which lay dormant in the soul? Was there some end sufficiently exalted to justify great undertakings and to deploy in all their splendor the faculties of mind and character with which man is endowed?

Many of my friends, I observed, were driven by this very need of finding some ideal, transcending personal pleasure, to which they could consecrate their lives. With more emotion than logic they prostrated themselves before the various human ideals which were in vogue. Some of them found satisfaction in devoting their energies to the progress of mankind, which they interpreted as the liberation of the toiling masses from the chains of capitalistic greed. Lacking religion, they bowed down to the imposing eschatology[3] of Marx, which, while neatly accounting for the all too evident misery of man, yet ministered to that hope for something better which ever burns within the human breast. While I envied the strength of their conviction and of their devotion, I considered the doctrines of these self-styled liberals both false and dangerous. In my heart I knew that the philosophy of Marx was wrong, because it took its departure from a false psychology. Having set out with an erroneous view of the human spirit – in effect, the classic hypothesis of economic man – Marx could never, I knew, make a correct analysis of the operations of that spirit in history or prescribe accurately the form which society should finally assume.

The psychology of the fascists, who had a very mediocre following at Harvard, impressed me as being somewhat sounder because it gave a place for love and sacrifice. But fascism's techniques of mob action, its dogmas of race and blood, and, above all, its exaltation of the State as the absolute good, were to me unacceptable. I remained untouched in my belief that the State was made for man, not man for the State.

Democracy, which I had previously assumed to be an unqualified blessing, began to appear under a less glistening aspect. By this I do not

---

3. The word eschatology may, I think, be used advisedly of a system which conceives of history as a monstrous dialectic of clashing interests tending constantly toward the final merger of the individual with the collective will, and looks toward the ultimate disappearance of caste rivalries in the static heaven of a classless society.

mean that I denied its purposes. I have always believed that the proper end of the State is to secure the well-being of all the people. But I refer to Democracy as an ideology, as the crude Nineteenth Century doctrine, nowhere completely put into practice, that the opinions and aspirations of the majority should determine the policies and actions of the State. That such government from below was a positive good I could not concede. At times, to be sure, it might be a necessary measure to protect the populace against the selfishness of a corrupt ruling class, but, ideally at least, the State should serve some higher purpose than to conform to the whims and illusions of the masses. Government, as I saw it, was a science having as its end the bodily and spiritual welfare of the whole community. Like other sciences, it required of its practitioners that they be loyal to its own object. Unbridled self-interest, in rulers as in private citizens, was a vice to be guarded against. But, and again like other sciences, government should be practiced by those who had the necessary learning and experience. In this I likened it to law and medicine. The argument that civil government, since it affected all, was everybody's business, impressed me little. Everyone, I replied, is interested in the good practice of medicine, but no one has seriously proposed that the manner of performing appendectomies should be made the object of a general referendum, or that M.D. degrees should be accorded by popular suffrage.

These political considerations may appear somewhat out of place in this essay, but I regard them as important in my religious development. In the first place, a little careful thought about such matters helped me to get over the juvenile notion that the individual must be the judge of all things. I saw that in questions of state, it was necessary to submit to the authority of qualified arbiters. I soon found myself at odds with those liberalistic forces, so prevalent at Harvard at the time, which were constantly making the "authoritarian" Catholic Church the butt of their invective. I, by contrast, became increasingly disposed to accept authority, not only in politics, but also in faith and morals.

I learned, also, the futility of trying to confer upon political ideologies that absolute loyalty which is paid to religious faith. I came to the view, which has remained with me ever since, that no particular form of government is a universal and unqualified good. Monarchies, oligarchies, and democracies – all are capable of being either efficient or corrupt. Systems of government, after all, are only so many methods of securing benefits to the governed. Much depends on what benefits are to be sought, for no one system is appropriate to every end. A society organized for war (for example, an army) should be differently constituted than a society consecrated to the blessings of peace. The particular social conditions must also be taken into account. Even the fondest zealots of democracy seemed to admit this by occasionally asserting that not all societies are "ripe" for self-government. To my mind, one of the great lessons of history was that royal and aristocratic societies, and even benevolent dictatorships, have at various times served to establish and maintain in a satisfactory degree the order, prosperity and liberty which most men lawfully desire. I could not, then, enroll myself under the banner of any particular political apostolate, and I distrusted the easy fanaticism with which some of my friends embraced certain ideals of government as if they were the sole font of salvation. They neglected to allow for diversities of social conditions and to consider seriously the ends for which governments are instituted. The purposes of human government, I perceived, were dependent on the purposes of human life. The latter must be discovered before the former could be intelligently discussed.

In my effort, then, to find some political ideal to which the whole man could be unreservedly dedicated, I was defeated. I was thrown back squarely on the moral and religious problem, which I had sought to avoid. The question, what is the final end of man, was abstruse and therefore unpleasant. But it called implacably for an answer. "Personal pleasure" I had already found inadequate as a goal. To erect in its place some abstract *summum bonum* was easy. Too easy because, unless more positive content were given to that formula, it did not answer either the moral problem or the personal need. To say the absolute good is the end in view of which all my actions must be ordered did not in itself establish any standard of conduct. Nor did the "absolute good," because of its abstract and impersonal nature, suffice to establish an adequate object on which to fix the energies of love, the impetus to serve and sacrifice, which were inescapably present in man.

In the darkness of my inner world the highest human instincts were confronted with a vacuum. Into that vacuum stepped the grace of God. The barren desolation of my materialist philosophy, its utter falseness and my humiliation at discovering it so, gave God His chance. The very extremeness of my error made conversion easier. Perhaps if I had had more specious beliefs and affections – some human idealism or some earthly loyalty – I might have been less willing to accept God's offering of Himself.

This offering occurred, suddenly and quite unexpectedly, on one grey February afternoon like many another. I was in Widener Library poring over a chapter of the *De civitate Dei* which had been assigned as reading in one of my courses in medieval history. On an impulse I closed the book; I was irresistibly prompted to go out into the open air. It was a bleak rainy day, rather warm for the time of year. The slush of melting snow formed a deep mud along the banks of the River Charles, which I followed down toward Boston. I enjoyed the cool rain in my face and the melancholy of the scene. As I wandered aimlessly, something impelled me to look contemplatively at a young tree. On its frail, supple branches were young buds attending eagerly the spring which was at hand. While my eye rested on them the thought came to me suddenly, with all the strength and novelty of a revelation, that these little buds in their innocence and meekness followed a rule, a law of which I as yet knew nothing. How could it be, I asked, that this delicate tree sprang up and developed and that all the enormous complexity of its cellular operations combined together to make it grow erectly and bring forth leaves and blossoms? The answer, the trite answer of the schools, was new to me: that its actions were ordered to an end by the only power capable of adapting means to ends – intelligence – and that the very fact that this intelligence worked toward an end implied purposiveness – in other words, a will. It was useless, then, to dismiss these phenomena by obscurantist talk about a mysterious force called "Nature." The "nature" which was responsible for these events was distinguished by the possession of intellect and will, and intellect plus will makes personality. Mind, then, not matter, was at the origin of all things. Or rather not so much the "mind" of Anaxagoras as a Person of Whom I had had no previous intuition.

Nor were the operations of this Person confined to flowers and foliage. The harmonious motions of the stars, the distribution of the elements, and the obedience of matter to fixed laws were manifestations of the same will and plan. Looking, then, into myself, I beheld energies coursing through the human person, the greater part of them beyond the realm of consciousness, tending constantly to preserve, to nourish, and to restore the weary body and soul. These forces were not of our own making, these operations not established by ourselves. Yet they had from their inception a legitimacy which was conferred upon them by Another – the same as Him Who moved the stars and made the lilacs bloom.

If, then, the very energies of growth and healing in the human body were hedged with sacredness, was it not monstrous that we, incapable of creating a hair, should undertake to dispose of our whole being, heedless of its appointed end? One had but to attend closely to the movements of the soul, when free from passion and from the self-induced blindness of perversity, to sense the marvelous harmony of all its tendencies, working in unison for the fulfillment in us of the divine purpose. Most of all was this true, as Plato and Aristotle had observed, of the spiritual faculties. The mind, as they had remarked, is naturally adapted toward knowledge and tends, unless obstructed, toward the apprehension of truth. The will, analogously, ever seeks the good and finds its fulfillment in ordering the lower parts of the soul according to the vision of the good which it beholds. To frustrate these tendencies, more native to us than ourselves, in a frenzied search of some arbitrary goal of our own choosing appeared in an unmistakable light to be blasphemous infraction of an eternal canon. Something sacred, I sensed, is violated, and a priceless opportunity irrevocably lost, when the mind is steeped in drunkenness and the will deprived of its energy, when lust for pleasure uses the mind as its instrument and debauches the effeminate will.

A glance at that great governing will and intellect which had given to all nature, the wide universe, its origin and end was a strong potion, awaking energies not easily harnessed or turned back. As I turned home that evening, the darkness closing round, I was conscious that I had discovered something which would introduce me to a new life, set off by a sharp hiatus from the past.

That night, for the first time in years, I prayed. I knelt down in the chill blackness at my bedside, as my mother had taught me to do when I was a little boy, and attempted to raise my heart and mind toward Him of Whose presence and power I had become so unexpectedly aware. I recited the Our Father. The words came slowly, and I had to make many new starts before the whole prayer unfolded itself in my mind. Our Father Who art in Heaven. Hallowed be Thy name. Thy will be done on earth, as it is in heaven. . . .

My first religious intimations, as the reader will observe, took on a Christian aspect. This Being Whom I perceived as the cause and consummation of the universe, the Alpha and Omega of all creation, was unmistakably the God of Christianity. He had nothing in common with the pagan myths of Zeus, of Thor, or of Brahma, about which I had read. He was not merely the abstract Good or Beautiful, nor was He the isolated Pure Act of Aristotle. He was Our Father Who had made us; He had a will which was done in heaven, but which we, with our selfish and perverse designs, were capable of frustrating, or at least of accomplishing in an unbefitting way.

At this point in my intellectual development — we have now arrived at the middle of my junior year in college — I had discovered several fundamental verities about the universe which served as the basis for a positive natural religion. In the first place, Plato had convinced me that good and evil were categories corresponding to objective realities, rather than mere fictions of the human mind. The Christian conception of God had perfected this Platonic intuition and infused it with a fresh vitality. As a result I saw beyond question that deliberately to obstruct the divine will, as manifested in nature, was absolutely and incontrovertibly evil. Conversely, to adhere to the divine purpose was, by objective and indubitable standards, good. I had, of course, no notion of the divine law except a natural one. I could see that the various organs of the body and soul had been established for definite ends. This fact was enough to establish the basic premise that moral values were something more than mere illusions.

Secondly, I saw that nothing was more to be done than the good, since the good, in its moral signification, is defined as that which ought to be done. In this conception, inchoate though it was, lay tremendous possibilities of development. Here at last was a Cause to which the entire man could be dedicated and a sure means of escaping the woeful emptiness of a life based merely on the avoidance of pain. Pleasure might in some way be related to the good – I was not to understand how until later – but I could be certain at least that the two were not identical. I saw the rectitude of Plato's view that he would rather be cast eternally into a pit in chains than commit an injustice. With pride I made that view my own.

But – and this is the specifically theistic element in my philosophy at the time – the good which I held to be supreme and worthy of all man's devotion was not an abstract ideal. It was a personal will, throbbing through the whole universe as the force which had created it, the power which sustained it in existence, and the goal toward which it tended. The moral good was merely an aspect of the Adorable Will of God. No abstract notion of the good could impress me as ultimate. The good was a value, and value implied appreciation, which is a function of personality. The good, conceived in personal terms, was capable of being made the object of loyalty and personal devotion. Dimly I saw that personality as such was higher than any lifeless thing, and that to serve or worship anything, be it concrete or abstract, which lacked intellect and volition, was to debase oneself and to desecrate the dignity of one's own being.

In the possession of this tripartite creed, made up of the existence of the moral law, its supremacy, and its relation to the will of God, I found a degree and quality of happiness which I had never before thought possible. The values which it established precluded any radical pessimism. Within its framework one could discover ends in terms of which one's actions could be purposively coordinated. Far as I was from the Catholic faith, the road now was a straight one. And philosophy had put me on that road.

I do not claim that I was or am or ever will be a philosopher in the sense of an expert on metaphysical questions. But in another sense anyone who stops to wonder what he should do or why he does that which he does must be a philosopher. He must formulate some guiding principles in terms of which he can make practical decisions. He must seek out the premises implied in his own actions and see to it that they are mutually consistent and theoretically sound.

Many persons pretend that philosophy is a dull study and one which has no relation to practical life. For me it has never been so. It was terribly clear to me from the beginning that I could not do anything — whether to help a friend in trouble, to eat a meal, or even to take a breath — without running the risk of being asked by some

Socrates, Why? What is the principle by which you justify this action? Does it ultimately tend to bring about that which you deem to be worth while? These questions haunted me, and I could have no peace until they had been answered. I would rather not act at all than act with the knowledge that I might better be doing nothing or doing the very opposite.

The man who refuses to face the philosophic problem is like a traveler in the night who will not take the time to decide where he is going because he is too much in a hurry to be on his way. He hastens first in one direction, then in the other, repeatedly striking his foot against cobblestones and stumbling in ruts, without approaching any nearer to his destination because he does not know whither he is bound. He becomes a slave to irrational impulses which incline him now this way and now that. Eventually he resolves that he will follow the crowd, but he has no way of telling whether they are proceeding to the same destination or whether they know where it is located. They disagree among themselves and he listens to their confused, discordant counsels. Finally he determines to follow the man who speaks in the loudest, most emphatic tones. When he has been led to one of those dead ends where error ends in impossibility he finds out to his grief that the ignorant prophet whom he had chosen to follow was one of those hireling leaders who speak with conviction in order to gratify a personal passion for having others follow them.

The general refusal of mankind to attempt to answer the questions raised by Socrates is perhaps the most dangerous folly in an age when folly seems to reign. The opinion that blind appetite could furnish a sufficient guide for action led to the general undermining of democracy. The consequent willingness of men to listen to any voice which spoke with accents of authority has permitted the establishment of unprecedented tyrannies. Man cannot with impunity continue to ignore philosophy. Happily, the actions of most of us are still superior to our philosophy. We are heirs to many of the conventions of Christianity, but most of us have put aside the articles of its creed. Ultimately, unless we restore our belief in God and our understanding of the moral law, the remainder of our Christian heritage will disintegrate. We will be left with naught but naked, savage cruelty. It is an ominous sign that great bodies of supposedly Christian persons have lately been seduced by myths of race and blood. And it is not impossible that the future holds yet darker errors.

The world needs philosophy, just as I needed it. Through a little elementary thinking about the purposes of our existence and the nature of the universe in which we live, we can prop up with reason the crumbling structure of our culture. If thought alone cannot bring us back to the faith of our ancestors, God grant that it may at least restore us to the level of ancient civilization and thus serve to stem the tidal wave of barbarism which threatens to engulf us.

A Testimonial
to Grace

2. The Divine Answer

The Divine Answer

Never, since the eventful day which I have described, have I doubted the existence of an all-good and omnipotent God. Proofs there were, and I had read them in the philosophy books. The proofs served to confirm and to clarify, but they could not have produced in its fullness my own conviction of the existence of God. All the proofs of God, precisely because they were proofs of something unseen, depended on the principle of sufficient reason. This principle, however well established, somehow failed to carry conviction to my mind. Certain in itself, it was not certain to me. Every rational demonstration seemed to leave room for just a particle of skepticism, which, as a result of man's natural disinclination to commit himself, could be turned to enormous account. My own acceptance of the existence of God rested on something more like an intuition. It was as though I had seen, at least for an instant, the divine power at work, infusing the whole universe with goodness and being. This intuition was by no means mystical, but it was a personal experience, and as such I find it partly incommunicable. I recorded it as best I can for whatever autobiographical interest it may have.

My path from this point to the Catholic Church was straight, as I have said, but it was long and steep. I did not become a Catholic until nearly two years later, after having begun my course at law school. My entire religious background was Protestant. My family on both sides had been Presbyterians for generations, and not one of my closer friends was a believing Catholic. In my existing environment I was almost completely isolated from Catholic doctrine, and a certain reticence, which I have never overcome, about discussing religious subjects, made it unthinkable at the time for me to enter a Catholic rectory for consultation with a priest. My religious intimations were at once too personal and too confused for vocal expression. The only conceptions which I had of the Catholic religion were those drawn from the teaching of Paul Doolin and a few scattered notions which I had gathered from my studies in medieval history.

It is not surprising, therefore, that I first thought of religion in Protestant terms.

The essential point is that I did think of religion. Indeed, in the time that was my own, I thought of almost nothing else. There was no question in my mind but that the only good worthy of the name was the praise and service of Almighty God. And I knew of no joy comparable with that of increasing one's understanding of the nature and operations of the Divine personality in Whom all goodness and truth and being had their source. "As the hart panteth after the

waterbrooks, so panteth my soul after the Lord."
That quotation could serve as the caption for the
next two years of my life.

Principally I found enlightenment concerning
the Divine personality in the Gospels. I made it
a rule – and one which I have found it harder to
break than to keep – that every night, no matter
how busy I might be, I would read at least one
chapter from the New Testament. I kept up this
custom for the next two years, never omitting a
night when it was possible for me to observe my
rule.

The words of Our Lord, as recorded in the
Gospels, rang with undeniable truth, but never
more so, to my mind, than when He insisted, as
He repeatedly did, on the knowledge and love of
God as the only things that mattered. Suffering
and persecution, He reiterated, were positive
blessings when endured for His sake. Religion
was the pearl of great price, the water which
alone could wholly quench our thirst; and He was
the way, the truth and the life. Far more clearly
than any man He taught that blessedness, not
pleasure, should be the object of our lives. This
was the doctrine for which I had been searching,
and I accepted it with joy.

Who was this Teacher, or better this Lover,
Who could not be restrained from giving until
the last drop of blood had left His martyred body?
Who was He, that He bade us so insistently to
follow Him, begged to refresh us with His doctrine

and to make us partakers of His joy? Was He, as He claimed, God and the Son of God?

After acquainting myself a little with the Gospels, I could have no patience with those modern writers and speakers who were incessantly trying to water down His "hard" doctrine, and to represent Christ Himself as a mild, tolerant and ever gentle moralist. I was impressed by His unsparing rage against the Pharisees and by His use of physical violence to cleanse the Temple from the moneychangers. I saw that He was a man Whom one could hate tremendously, as most of His contemporaries did hate Him, for what they took to be his bad manners and extravagant ideas. The thought occurred to me that most of those who attempted to make Christ seem so moderate and "respectable" would have hated and feared Him had they known Him as He was.

Christ, as He appeared in the Scriptures, was not primarily a moralist. For conduct as such He cared relatively little; love and faith He cherished above measure. His teaching took the form, not of dry aphorisms like those of Confucius or Poor Richard, but of parables charged with the poetry of life. These parables were so direct that the most unlettered could grasp their message. At the same time they were so rich in doctrine and symbolism that the most learned could not exhaust their subtle moral implications, their wealth of dogma and their deep prophetic meaning. The moralists never seemed to rise above the obvious. Christ never paused to state the obvious. He told of things no man had seen.

Nor was He merely a philosopher, another Socrates or Plotinus. They, after long inductive processes, came to tentative conclusions about the nature of God, the immortality of the soul, and the good life. Christ, Who seemed a stranger to discursive thought, spoke readily and with finality about these matters. He could use keen logic, and often did so to confute the Scribes and Pharisees, but His knowledge of spiritual matters was direct and immediate. His doctrine, higher than that of the philosophers, did not have the same source.

But could not Christ be classed as a religious fanatic, like Mohammed for example? To compare Him with the frenzied Arab epileptic was outright blasphemy.[1] His judgment, unlike that of the fanatics, was always calm and clear, and His perception of His environment complete and penetrating. His doctrine, moreover, was thoroughly consistent with itself and with the facts of nature. When the philosophers later made it their study they found that the Christian faith enabled them to see clearly what Plato and Aristotle had hesitantly inferred. Once Christ had lived, Western philosophy could never be the

---

1. [This estimation of Mohammed is one that I would not be prepared to defend. On the assumption that it was probably a polemical distortion I omitted any reference to Mohammed as an epilectic in the Italian and Spanish translations of 1959 and 1963, respectively.]

same again. Mohammed had had no comparable influence on Arabic philosophy.

Was it possible, then, that Christ was more than a man? I investigated the arguments for His divinity, and found them no less cogent for being conventional. First, there was an embarrassing frequency of miracles in all the accounts of Christ. If He had performed any of them, He might well have performed all. He was neither a charlatan nor a fool, yet He repeatedly claimed miraculous powers, and, if the accounts had any normal degree of veracity, demonstrated that power again and again. The doctrine of the Gospels was sublime, and was indubitably a faithful account of Christ's teaching. To whom else could one accredit it? But was the view tenable that the miracles were something superadded by ignorant and credulous disciples? In Lionel Curtis' *City of God* I had read an able presentation of that thesis, but I found it unacceptable. Christ's doctrine was inseparably wedded to His miracles. Time and again He had illustrated His doctrine by His miracles and invoked His miracles as proof of His doctrine. One had to take both or neither. If, then, the Gospel accounts of Christ's doctrine were authentic – as I could not but concede – the miracles also must be accepted. Mr. Curtis, I felt, was not meeting the facts squarely. He was tailoring them to fit the frame of his own narrow rationalism.

One miracle which stood up to every test was the Resurrection. Any attempt to dismiss it as a hallucination was useless. That thousands of persons should have suffered a hallucination extending over a period of forty days was harder to account for than the Resurrection itself. Was it, then, a clever trick of Christ or His disciples? Nothing could have been more unlike Christ than to masquerade as a walking corpse in order to deceive His followers. And nothing could have been more unlike the disciples, who had weakly denied Christ in His Passion, than to go out and die for a myth of their own coinage.

The most persuasive proof of all for me was the way in which this risen Christ acted. What literary artist could have thought up such conversations as Christ held when He said Mass for the pilgrims at Emmaus ("Did not our hearts burn within us as He spoke?"),[2] when He convinced the doubting Thomas, and when He commissioned Saint Peter to feed His sheep? In all these incidents one senses unmistakably the personality of Christ. The very detail is evidence of a sane and honest witness. It is even recorded that He ate broiled fish and honeycomb. If an accomplished novelist could not have invented all this, how could a group of lying or demented fishermen have done so?

---

2. [In speaking of the Supper at Emmaus as a Mass I go beyond the textual evidence, but the Eucharistic overtones of the incident, as recounted in Luke's Gospel, are unmistakable. In the Italian and Spanish translations I changed the text to read that Jesus broke bread with these disciples.]

Further testimony of the divinity of Christ was contained in the Prophecies. It seemed at least a peculiar coincidence that this righteous, wise, and powerful Person, Whose works and teachings themselves suggested that He was more than a man, should have been born, not a Greek or a Roman, but a Jew — a member of that race which had cherished from time immemorial the promise of a Messias. Still more remarkable did it appear that Jesus was conceived in the manner predicted of the Redeemer, born in the prescribed village, and that He suffered in every detail the afflictions and death foretold of the Messias.

The wicked Herod, the holy Simeon, and a handful of others were alone in recognizing the applicability of the Prophecies. The priests and Pharisees utterly misconstrued them, and so likewise did the disciples when they took scandal at His death. Yet the Scriptures were strangely accurate. How eloquently the dolorous Passion had been depicted in the Psalms: "All they that see Me laugh Me to scorn . . . They pierced My hands and My feet: they have numbered all My bones. They look and stare upon Me. They part My garments among them, and upon My vesture they cast lots." The Psalms were filled with similar predictions, and likewise the Book of Jeremias, but none had foreseen so accurately as Isaias, and in such marvelous detail, the birth, life, and death of Our Lord. His writings abounded in startling prognostications: "Behold a virgin shall conceive . . .," "All ye that pass by the way attend and see . . .,"[3] "There is no beauty in Him nor comeliness . . ." Was it not possible that in these and other texts, unsurpassed in literary merit, the Holy Ghost had revealed to the ancient seers the life of Him upon Whom they set their hopes? Indeed it seemed likely that Christ was the promised Savior of Whom they had written.

If the Messianic commission of Christ was attested by the Prophecies, the same could equally well be said of the Figures, in which Christ was foreshadowed not in thought only, but in deed. I was deeply impressed by the mysterious symbolism which penetrated the actions of Noe, Isaac, Moses, Jonas, Melchisedech, and the other precursors of Christ. Most apt of all the Figures, to my mind, was the Joseph episode. The most beloved of Jacob's sons, he arouses the jealousy of his brothers. They equivalently put him to death and entomb him in a pit. He rises from the pit and goes before them into a far country. A famine occurs, and the family of Joseph are forced, with the humility of the Prodigal Son, to beg sustenance from him whom they had thought to kill and who now reigns in a land of abundance. On discovering his identity, his brothers fear for their lives. He forgives them, however, and bestows upon them far more than they had dared to ask. Written many centuries before Christ's

---

3. [The quotation "All ye that pass . . ." is actually from the Lamentations of Jeremiah. The other quotations are, as stated, from Isaiah. In the Italian and Spanish translations a reference to Jeremiah is introduced at this point.]

birth, the story of Joseph was a perfect parable of His death and resurrection.

Indeed, I observed, the entire Old Testament could be read as an allegory of the New. Every sacrifice offered up by the priests and patriarchs under the Old Law was an inadequate effort to accomplish in advance the Paschal sacrifice of Christ, the Lamb of God. Every aspiration to reach the Promised Land was a mystical striving to force the gates of heaven, which were to be opened by Christ. The works and sufferings of the ancient Prophets could not be properly interpreted except in terms of the coming of Him to whom their hearts incessantly went forth, "the desire of the everlasting hills."

The Messianic character of Christ's mission appeared not only in these adumbrations of His coming, but equally in the events which filled His life as He walked on earth. His personal eminence as a teacher and as a virtuous man paled to insignificance beside the vicarious role which He played as Victim and Redeemer. He was the second Adam, the progenitor of grace, and was destined, through the fruit of the Tree of the Cross, to repair the damage wrought by the first Adam in partaking of the fruit of the forbidden Tree.

Every incident in the life of Christ was intimately linked with His redemptive mission. Each of His miracles, I perceived, illustrated in a particular way His relation to the entire human species in the order of grace. When He changed the water into wine at Cana, for example, He was not merely performing a courteous service to relieve His host's embarrassment. The wine which He gave to the marriage guests was symbolic of His own Advent when the sources of prophetic wisdom seemed to have run dry. More precisely, that exquisite wine could be interpreted as signifying the Precious Blood which He was to shed for mankind on the altar of the Cross. Again, when Our Lord satisfied the hunger of the five thousand on the mountain, He mystically anticipated the immolation of His Body on Calvary, explicitly declaring at the time, "The bread that I will give is My flesh." Similarly, when, after the Resurrection, He brought in the miraculous draft of fishes, He was not merely giving evidence of His divine power or ministering to the material needs of His disciples: He was demonstrating to Peter how great a multitude of souls He would later draw into the Church. The event must be understood in terms of the words, "Behold, I will make you fishers of men." The extraordinary strength of the net, which causes the Evangelist to remark that it did not break, is an indication of the indivisibility of the Church.

In the whole of Christ's earthly sojourn, I perceived, there is not one occurrence, however trivial in appearance, which does not take on momentous proportions in terms of His capacity as Messias. Each event tends to confirm and to clarify His cosmic mission. Nothing is left to chance: a dramatic necessity presides over all. In one way or another every circumstance serves to establish more positively Christ's supernatural role as an acceptable oblation for man's sin.

Even his enemies assist Our Lord to become the protagonist of this colossal drama of reparation. The anguish and contumely which they rudely heap upon Him are the predestined lot of one who is to be offered up to the Father as an immaculate victim. The callous indifference of the enrollees who had congregated at Bethlehem excluded Our Lady from the hospitality of the inn, and brought upon Our Lord the humble circumstances of His Birth. The jealousy of Herod made Him an exile from the first moment of His childhood. The hypocrisy of the Pharisees compelled Him to live His public life as an outcast and a wanderer. The avarice of Judas, the worldliness of Pontius Pilate, and the savage inconstancy of the populace prepared His mournful Passion and staged the ignominy of His triumph. The irony of the events is unparalleled: the unconscious adoration of Pilate in crowning Christ's head with thorns and in pinning the royal inscription on the Cross; the raucous crying of the Jews, "We will have no king but Caesar . . . His blood be upon us and upon our children." How terribly history was to fulfill that optative when Jerusalem was sacked and the Temple destroyed! How beautifully history would fufill it yet again when that same blood descended on Christ's kinsmen to redeem them!

Here was a drama more perfect than if it had been humanly planned. Yet the actors were real men, unconscious of their roles. What better proof could there be than this of Christ's supernatural destiny as the Messias of the Jews and the Redeemer of mankind?

Probable indeed it was that Christ was the Divine Being Whom He claimed to be. But probability was not enough. Christ asked us to consent to give up everything and follow Him, and this one could not rationally do on the basis of mere probability. It was necessary to put away every doubt and to commit oneself without reservation. Christ constantly insisted on this act of unqualified faith as an essential step. Even the love of which He spoke was a love founded on faith. Merely sentimental affection was insufficient. That which would be so amply rewarded was not the act of giving a cup of water to the least of men: it was doing so for Christ's sake.

Before I could make this final act of faith, a full year and a half were to elapse after I had accepted the divinity of Christ as probable. Saint Matthew had not taken five minutes to make a total surrender! Trained as I was in the habits of skepticism, the act of faith was for me a terrible stumbling block. In a sense it seemed to be the surrender of that which I valued more than anything else: intellectual honesty. To make a subjective certainty out of an objective probability was a sacrifice of reason itself. Yet, paradoxically, it was a reasonable sacrifice: for how else could one consent to follow Christ with that singleness of devotion which He, as God, could rightfully exact?

That I did eventually make this act of faith is attributable solely to the grace of God. I could never have done so by my own power. The grace which I received was a tremendous and unmerited privilege, but I sincerely believe that it is one which God, in His faithfulness, will deny to none who earnestly seeks Him in prayer. I found Him to be exactly as Our Lord had described Him — a Father Who would not give a stone in place of bread, or anything but the Holy Ghost to those who asked for It. "Knock, and it shall be opened unto you."

The same thirst for a fuller knowledge of God's nature and of His will for men which induced me to search the Scriptures impelled me also to look to the churches for guidance. As I became more familiar with the personality and doctrine of Our Divine Lord, I felt the need for some living institution which would bring Christ closer as a Person and apply His lofty principles to the circumstances of this remote age. I began attending religious services regularly, often twice on Sunday, in the hope of finding some preacher who, aware of the radical content of Christ's message, would present it in vivid and concrete terms. My ideas about life had changed radically, and I wanted to be told how I should reform my actions in order to make them consistent with my new beliefs.

I went to Protestant churches of nearly every denomination – Presbyterian, Episcopalian, Methodist, Baptist, Unitarian, and nonsectarian. In none of these did I find what I was looking for. Whatever the individual differences between these sects might be, they were alike, in the manifestations which I saw of them, in failing to insist on the inerrancy of the doctrine which they had inherited from Christ. The ministers were content to be accorded a merely human and provisional authority. They required no explicit and definite profession of faith. The Apostles' Creed was chanted emptily, as if its content were of no importance. The injunctions of Christ were handled as lightly as quotations from Shakespeare and Carlyle. Lay poets and essayists were repeatedly invoked as lending authority to divine revelation. Every member of the congregation was considered entitled to interpret as strictly or as loosely as he pleased the word of God.

Christ Himself was frequently discussed on a merely human level. He was congratulated for His psychological insight, for His artful leadership, and even for His sense of humor. His Messianic role, on the other hand, was deliberately ignored, and the dogmatic aspects of His teaching were casually passed over. More often than not, His doctrine about hell was soft-pedaled as though it might perhaps be a little out of date. Reference to the miraculous and to the order of grace was generally avoided. The sermons given in these churches were for the most part little more than homely disquisitions on self-improvement, punctuated with literary aphorisms and allusions to current events.

Rarely did these pulpit-lecturers invite one to drink from the chalice of Christ's Passion. Theirs was not the intense personal faith for which the martyrs had shed their blood. Rather than pointing to the way of suffering and sacrifice, they dwelt almost exclusively on the psychological benefits and the interior consolation to be derived from religion. They failed to emphasize that radical inversion of human values which had been wrought by the Cross on which Christ died. Instead, they appealed primarily to human wisdom and to humanitarian sentiment. All this they could have done quite as effectively if the bloody holocaust of Calvary had never been accomplished.

Disillusioned with the Protestant churches, I determined to find out what Catholicism had to offer. One day I went to Mass. If there be anyone who contends that in order to be converted to the Catholic faith one must be first attracted by the beauty of the liturgy, he will have me to explain away. Filled as I was with a Puritan antipathy toward splendor in religious ritual, I found myself actually repulsed by the elaborate symbolism in which the Holy Sacrifice is clothed. Having been nourished for years upon the illusion of a Divine Master enamored of stoic simplicity,

I felt that the display of embroidered vestments and gilded chalices was fundamentally incompatible with the spirit of true worship. The scent of incense, to my mind, represented anything rather than devout prayer. The painted statuary I viewed, not with the eye of one seeking communion with the saints, but with the sternly critical regard of one visiting a museum of art. More than I realized, I was on the watch for the bogey of "Romanist idolatry." While the quality of attention which prevails in Catholic churches during Mass is in truth a remarkable, and practically unique, phenomenon, it was one which eluded me entirely. In their thoughts, nearly all present were deeply aware of the invisible drama unfolding itself on the altar; but there was little external unity to be discerned. The priest, so far from telling the congregation when to sit or stand or kneel, carried out his tasks almost as though he were alone. The congregation, for their part, were not watching with scrupulous exactitude the movements of the celebrant. Some, on the contrary, were reciting prayers on mysterious strings of beads, which Catholics call rosaries. Others were thumbing through pages of prayer-books and Missals, which, for all I knew, might have been totally unrelated to the Mass. Not even a hymn was sung to bring unity into this apparently dull and disconnected service. The sermon – the only thing I understood was dry in content and dryly delivered. It was however, based firmly on the premise that Christ was God and His teaching the revealed word of God.

The most interesting feature of this experiment is that, while the Protestant churches left me with a sense of mere inadequacy, the Catholic Church I found in many respects positively repellent. I stubbornly resisted the emotion which swept through the edifice at the moment of the Transubstantiation; I refused to be taken in by the candles, the vestments, and the incense; I positively recoiled from images of the Sacred Heart immersed in flames, and felt a stern contempt for Catholic religious art in general. I preferred the cold chastity of Protestant worship.

This revulsion on my part I attribute not merely to the strangeness of the rite and to the Puritan bias with which I was affected, but also to a personal unwillingness to succumb to any religious emotion before I had answered intellectually the religious problem. I was determined not to let sentiment draw reason in its wake. Whether in choosing reason I chose the better guide I am not certain. Man's natural religious inclinations often bring him more readily to the truth than his intelligence, which is easily ensnared. There are many approaches by which God can lead souls to the Catholic faith. Mine was only one, and perhaps not the best. Some time passed before I again crossed the threshold of a Catholic church, and a great deal longer before I acquired an appreciation of the exceptional beauty of Catholic ecclesiastical ceremonies. In my senior year at college I began attending High Mass regularly on Sundays, and gradually mastered the complexities of the Roman Missal. Better still, I came to understand the action of the Mass, apart from which its trappings are meaningless and even, to some, distasteful. That year I assisted with great devotion at nearly all the special Lenten services, and was deeply moved by the chanting of Tenebrae. The most thrilling experience of the year was perhaps Holy Saturday, when I rose at five-thirty in the morning to witness in full the blessing of the New Fire, of the Paschal Candle, and of the Baptismal Font, together with the recitation of the Prophecies, the celebration of Holy Mass, and the singing of Vespers. These observances, however, were scarcely instrumental in causing my conversion, for I was already at that time a Catholic in opinion. Only the decisive act of faith was wanting.

Not until I had actually made my profession of faith did I yield to the attraction of Catholic devotional art, which I now regard as a most singular aid to prayer and contemplation. Nothing serves better than visual representation to make us aware of the presence of God and of our communion with the saints, who ever lovingly intercede for us. Once faith has gone before, there can be no excess of religious emotion, provided that it be of the right quality. One can not help regretting, in this connection, that sugary sentimentality has gained so large a place in Catholic religious art, perhaps as a reaction against the systematic coldness of Jansen and the Protestant Reformers. I hope, however, that a counter-reaction will not result in a form of art which ceases to emphasize the human tenderness of Our Lord and of the saints. In religious art, I have learned, devotional values properly take precedence over purely esthetic considerations.

Catholic religious forms and ceremonies, then, were of little importance in effecting my conversion. Far different, however, was the effect of my explorations in the field of theology. I read extensively in this branch of literature and discovered that theological principles were the sole secure foundation on which to base moral decisions, doctrinal tenets, and religious sentiment. Catholic theology is an immensely impressive structure, as few who are familiar with it can candidly deny. The men who developed its vast and carefully chiselled framework in the Middle Ages were professional philosophers in a sense in which John Dewey, Bertrand Russell, and even Alfred Whitehead — to name but three of the prophets of our day — are not. They did not leap suddenly from the pond of psychology or of mathematics into the vast sea of metaphysics. Their minds had been sharpened by years of the most rigorous discipline before their apprenticeship was deemed complete. Each of them, moreover, took up where his master had left off, so that scholastic theology was the composite product of many of the best trained philosophic minds which mankind has ever known. They saw far because they were not too proud to sit on the shoulders of giants.

Reading even the history of scholastic thought, as presented by such able modern exponents as Maurice de Wulf, Étienne Gilson, and Paul Vignaud, was a veritable religious experience, so splendid a light did it cast on the moral law and on the nature of God and the universe. Gradually, and after centuries of the most penetrating analysis, the infinite justice of God was shown to be compatible with His unbounded charity, and the sufficiency of faith was harmonized with the necessity for good works. Human freedom was skillfully reconciled with the fulness of the divine foreknowledge, and the goodness and omnipotence of God with the imperfection of the created world. Believing in order that they might understand, the medieval doctors discovered that understanding made believing easy. Their wisdom provided the nourishment on which my faith grew strong.

From modern presentations I went back to primary sources. My mind rejoiced in the bold eloquence of Saint Augustine and in the lucidity of Saint Thomas Aquinas, in the sublimity of Saint Bonaventure and in the shrewd penetration of Duns Scotus. Concurrently, I read some of the Catholic philosophers of our own day, including Father D'Arcy, Father Martindale, and E. I. Watkin. In them also I noted that seasoned comprehension and serenity of outlook which characterized the great tradition of Catholic thought. I perused nearly all the published writings of Jacques Maritain, and was startled by his brilliant insight, from the vantage-point of his religious faith, into social, esthetic, and metaphysical questions.

I listened to the public addresses of Monsignor Sheen, and in them I found expressed that boldly Christian view of man and the modern world for which I had sought in vain in the Protestant churches. My non-Catholic friends whom I introduced to the oratory of Monsignor Sheen were horrified that I should be seduced by such an outright demagogue. They protested that he did not give sufficient credit to the opposition, that he oversimplified philosophic problems, that he proved too much from too little. But I was not looking for airtight logical proofs; I was looking for a priest and a prophet. I was looking, if you like, for a practical, living proof that intelligent men in our day could regard the supernatural, the miraculous as a fact of experience without having to apologize to anyone for this conviction. I wanted evidence that faith and prayer could penetrate beneath the confused surface of economics and history to the realm where the powers of light and darkness clash in unceasing strife. Father Sheen demonstrated to me that the Catholic Church could still sustain and nourish the unfeigned charity and the burning conviction of the first Apostles, qualities which appeared to be all but extinct in the contemporary world. He taught me little about philosophy which I had not already suspected; but he taught me a great deal about the ways of God to man and gave me confidence in the religious conclusions which I had fumblingly reached through my own explorations. Jacques Maritain and Fulton Sheen, more than any other two writers, provided me with a new social philosophy, suited to the metaphysics of Aristotle and of the Christian tradition, and capable of supplanting in my mind the political liberalism which corresponded with the metaphysics which I had come to reject. They made known to me the Encyclical letters of Leo XIII and Pius XI, in which the content of Catholic social teaching was so admirably summarized.

My previous opinion that the best government is that which governs least was, I noted, based on the philosophical postulates of liberalism. Liberalism, if it implies anything at all, implies the cult of liberty – the liberty of the individual person from various restraining influences.[4] The liberals considered that all virtue and progress were conditioned primarily upon freedom. To advance, they maintained, it sufficed that one should be free to act without reference to the directions of others. The heritage of the past was glibly dismissed as a dead hand, and

---

4. Here, and throughout the next few pages, I attempt to depict the pure type of liberalism, as it appeared to me during my collegiate days. I am well aware that, however broadly liberalism be defined, there will be some so-called "liberals" whose doctrines do not fall within the scope of the definition.

the authority of the living denounced as an onerous yoke. Liberty, it was recognized, is conducive to change; and change, being deified, was identified with progress. The Nineteenth Century idea of progress was, in the field of historical criticism, the logical counterpart of the liberal conception of man and society.

In their doctrine of the person, the liberals borrowed extensively from the philosophical premises of Kant and Hegel, who had themselves leaned heavily on the political prophet of liberalism, Rousseau. The individual was represented as a morally and juridically sovereign unit, as an inviolable citizen of the anarchic "Kingdom of Ends." The more extreme idealists went so far as to place within each human spirit the ultimate source of all right, reality, and truth.

Each person being accounted an end in himself, it followed that society was an artificial assemblage of self-contained individuals, unconnected by any functional interrelationship. Both in fact and in theory, communal life became increasingly acephalous and atomistic. The subordination of man to man was decried as an intrinsic evil, and the natural diversities which cause men to be dependent upon one another were deliberately ignored. It was considered essentially degrading to be placed in a position of service to another; God was said to favor those who helped *themselves*. Any virtues which did not find their final cause within the individual fell into scorn and disrepute: humility, meekness, obedience, and fidelity were said to be the marks of feeble and dependent natures. Conversely, virtues such as self-reliance and initiative were inordinately exalted. The concept of human equality was indiscriminately applied to all matters. The political and social status of women was not differentiated from that of men.

The family, like other social relationships, was reduced to a mere legalistic partnership. The differences of function between its several members were blurred, and the authority of the father as the natural head of the household undermined. Marriage was represented as a bilateral contract terminable at the will of either party.

The political tenets of liberalism, like its social philosophy, reflected a gross overemphasis on the autonomy of the human person. Each individual being considered a distinct sovereignty, the very existence of the State could hardly be justified. Some theorists maintained that all government was a mere imposition, and the best government that which governed least. Others attempted to salvage the rights of the State by depicting it as an expression of the united will of its constituent members. According to Hegel, the policies of the State mystically embodied the "higher" will of the citizens, and consequently were not amenable to criticism. Rousseau, Mill, and the preponderant body of liberal philosophers, despite certain inconsistencies in their pronouncements, ordinarily vindicated the authority of the State by ascribing its origin to a supposed contract in which all the members had implicitly concurred. Yet sovereignty, it was affirmed, still abided in the individual to such a degree that each citizen, no matter how ignorant he might be (short of actual insanity), possessed an intrinsic right to be heard, directly or through his elected representatives, on every question of law or policy. He could not, according to the majority of liberal thinkers, be bound by any measure in the adoption of which he had not had a voice. Self-determination, almost to the exclusion of other factors, was made the guiding principle for settling, not only the internal affairs of states, but also the extent of their respective domains.

In opposition to this autonomism, the Catholic Church proposed a social philosophy predicated on a different and profounder analysis of the human person. While recognizing and respecting freedom of choice, the Church denied that human freedom was tantamount to complete self-determination. Man, it was pointed out, is dependent on his neighbor for both his survival and his development. Born into the world in a condition of extreme helplessness, he never becomes sufficient unto himself, nor is it desirable that he should do so. The family, then, is a natural unit, sanctioned by the reciprocal interdependence of its members. Larger social units, likewise, are natural and organic; and civil government is a necessary institution willed by God and required by nature for the maintenance of order within the community. The State is a sovereign entity charged with assuring in the temporal order the tranquillity, prosperity, and equity necessary for the proper fulfillment by its members of their respective destinies as human persons. A government, to be legitimate, need not in every instance be established by the voluntary action of the governed; and laws, for their validity, depend not so much on the concurrence of the governed as on their inherent justice. In the State, as a body corporate, the various members have their distinct functions, contributing in various ways to the well-being of the whole. To some the function of determining policies is specially appropriated; to others, that of implementing them. Some perform offices of greater dignity, and receive greater honors, than their fellows; but all, as human persons, have certain inalienable rights. The inequalities and differences which obtain in every organized community are as healthy as they are inevitable. And where a perfectly flexible social system can not be achieved, the "vocation" of the individual will, it was observed, be in some measure determined by the circumstances of his birth. The good life is compatible with a relatively humble position in the social scale.

The liberals, confusing novelty with progress, desired that each individual person should arrive at his convictions by means of original thought, and were exceedingly reluctant to admit that any particular truth, being founded on objective reality, was incumbent upon all. So disproportionately did they emphasize the importance of the material factors of "race, time, and circumstance" that it was seriously contended that what was true on this side of the Alps might be false on the other. In their flight from dogmatism, the liberals rejected all stable principles, and sought to make absolutes out of doubt, diversity, and change. Some adherents of the liberal school merely professed skepticism as to the capacity of the human mind to attain objective truth; others contended that truth itself was relative to the individual mind. The idealists went so far as to affirm that both truth and reality were subjectively immanent within the human spirit. Even those liberals who allowed that there was such a thing as objective error were unwilling to concede that it should be suppressed. The individual, they proclaimed, had an inviolable right to give unrestricted expression to his opinions, no matter how absurd or dangerous they might be. The propagation of falsehood they defended, either on the naïve assumption that men in general would see the truth more clearly when the correlative error was placed in juxtaposition (Mill), or on the cynical assumption that, so far as society is concerned, truth can be attained only under the form of a "counterbalancing of contrary errors" (Acton). In contrast to this teaching, Catholicism proposed a theory which, while encouraging the expression of original thought in matters which are properly the subject of opinion, safeguarded the integrity of those truths which were objectively certain in the light of natural reason or of divine Revelation, and were salutary for all.

In its educational philosophy, liberalism insisted constantly on the free expansion of the individual soul, as a sovereign and autonomous unit, according to its own inclinations. The benefits of acquired knowledge were cast aside, and each student was urged to discover, through his own efforts, his personal brand of "truth." Discipline and indoctrination were deplored; self-expression extolled beyond measure. As a result, the individual was left without principles, without character, and without moral stamina. In the progressive schools was fulfilled the prophecy of Plato: "The master fears and flatters his scholars, and the scholars despise their masters and tutors" (*Republic*).

Catholicism, on the other hand, without neglecting the importance of individual initiative, emphasized the role of external guidance in the formation of mind and character. The value of an opinion, it was remarked, derived not from its originality so much as from its veracity. Conformity with objectively evident standards of thought and conduct, it was maintained, should rightly be expected of all.

Unwilling to admit the existence of objective canons of justice, the liberals reduced all law to a matter of expediency. The State in their philosophy was confined to functioning as a mediator between the conflicting interests of rival social blocs. Law was regarded as a regrettable, if necessary, restriction on the freedom of individuals to do as they pleased. The very fact that it tended to assure order was considered proof that it impeded progress. Law was divorced and segregated from morality, the sphere of the latter being made purely interior and subjective. The light of the individual conscience was urged as the sole criterion of ethical right and wrong, and the categorical imperative, existing within the mind, was commonly invoked as the unique guide of consciences. Catholicism, by contrast, offered a theory of law consonant with the notion that justice and morality are objective values; that their principles are knowable – and to a large degree known – in the light of Revelation and of natural reason. The dignity of law, as the embodiment and guarantor of justice, was emphasized. The State, according to Catholic theory, had a positive duty to see that each obtained his due.

The economics of liberalism rested on the optimistic assumption that if every individual is granted unlimited freedom to gratify his personal desire for wealth, a maximum of prosperity for all will be the result. In the name of free enterprise, private lust for gain was permitted to override the most elemental human rights, and labor was treated as a marketable commodity. Production became no longer an exercise of art, but a mere expression of greed. In contrast to this theory, Catholicism urged an economic philosophy based on the primacy of human and spiritual values. The State was accorded a responsibility for coordinating economic undertakings so as to assure the benefit of all concerned. The dignity of labor and the consequent entitlement of laborers to form mutually protective associations were boldly affirmed in opposition to the exponents of *laissez-faire* capitalism. Private property was recognized as a right normally appertaining to the human person, and the inequity of a system which tends to concentrate wealth in the hands of a very few was fearlessly exposed.

In all these aspects of social philosophy, I found that the Catholic Church offered a vigorous and coherent critique of liberalism. Liberalism I was bound to reject because I had repudiated the individualism, the relativism, and the subjectivism on which it was predicated. I could no longer temporize with a system which at every point tended to substitute doubt for faith, pleasure for hope, and egoism for charity. Communism and fascism I had found intellectually sterile and in practice pernicious. Catholicism, on the other hand, possessed an admirably clear and progressive social teaching consistent with a sound metaphysics and with a Christian view of the universe. To the Church I was bound to go not only for my metaphysics but even for my social philosophy.

Admiration for Catholic philosophy, however, was a very different thing from submission to the authority of the Church. Conceivably one might be able to accept the greater part of the Catholic teaching concerning man and society and yet re-

main an independent thinker, without any particular religious affiliation. But I personally, as
I have indicated above, felt urgently impelled
toward a closer communion with Christ – toward
a more concrete participation in the fruits of the
Redemption – than I could derive from reading
and thought, or even from prayer. Christ as an
idea was not enough. I desired to know Him as
a tangible reality.

Our Lord had not been content to come to
mankind under a purely spiritual aspect, fitting
as it might have seemed for Him to do so. He had
not presented His elect with a perfect book and
taken His departure. He had come in the flesh
to the children of men and had stayed to walk
before their eyes. He had thought it worthwhile
to suffer as a man – to feel hunger, thirst, fatigue
and physical pain. By His presence and example
He had strengthened and encouraged His disciples. With lips of flesh and blood He had dispelled
their doubts and fears. He had condescended to
become a visible object of human devotion. He
had permitted His sacred feet to be cleansed by
the Magdalen's repentant tears, His holy countenance to be wiped by the gentle Veronica's precious veil,[5] and His lifeless limbs to be held by

---

5. [The Italian translator of the orginal version of this book
   asked and obtained my permission to omit the phrase
   referring to Veronica because he feared that it could support
   superstition. When I wrote these words I was still struggling
   against unbelief, and was relatively unconcerned with the
   problem of superstition. The translator, however, was correct
   in pointing out the lack of biblical and historical evidence

Mary His mother within her arms when the last agony was over. With human words He had forgiven sins and with a human touch He had restored health to the infirm.

From me, however, Christ was remote. He was a figure in history who had died, arisen, and disappeared. It was as though the Word had been incarnate for a handful of men only, in the distant past.

Yet He had said that He would not leave us orphans. He had promised to remain in our midst. "Behold," He had said, "I am with you all days, even to the consummation of the world." Between Him and me two thousand years had run their course. What could bridge that gulf? A Church, if there was one, in which Christ continued visibly His ministry on earth.

Christ had founded such a Church. The Gospel was explicit. Because of your faith, He had said to Saint Peter, I will build My Church on you, and it shall never fail. I commission you to feed My sheep in My absence. For a lifetime only? No, surely for all posterity. To the Apostles He had said, I charge you with teaching all nations, baptizing them in the name of the Father, of the Son, and of the Holy Ghost. I will send the Holy Ghost to guide you, so that your teaching may be infallible. The sins which you forgive on earth will be forgiven in heaven. Continue to enact the

---

for the Veronica incident. The Spanish translation retains the reference to Veronica.]

sacrifice of My Body and Blood: he who eats My Body and drinks My Blood will be saved.

Christ, then, had not omitted to supply this fundamental need of human nature. When He left us, He appointed representatives to answer men's questions concerning faith and morals and to carry on His sanctifying work on earth, forgiving sins, administering the cleansing waters of Baptism, and distributing the Body which He had immolated for us on the Cross. With His deep understanding of mankind, He had inaugurated visible rites and had chosen to confer invisible graces by means of them. It was thoroughly characteristic of Our Lord to require us to do small physical acts evidencing a little faith and a little humility, and then to recompense them with enormous spiritual rewards. It was part of the logic of the Incarnation that He should give Himself to us in Holy Communion, not only by spiritual indwelling in the soul, but sensibly under the appearances of the bread and wine. With ineffable joy I read that He had actually done so: that the Word had been made flesh not only for Peter and James and John, but for all posterity. One could still adore God visibly in the Eucharist. One could still be united physically to His Sacred Person — both human and divine — more closely (in a sense) than was Our Lady when she had carried the Infant Jesus in her womb.

Now indeed did my soul, like that of the Psalmist, faint in the courts of the Lord. The very pace and movement of the heart were altered with desire for its absent Lord. Not the heart only, but the whole body through which the heart's pulse flowed, was penetrated with the sense of exile and of longing for Him of Whom it had been told. The ears were impatient to hear the sound of His voice saying through the lips of His appointed priest, "Arise and go in peace; thy sins are forgiven thee." The eyes cared to look upon naught else if they could not behold Him in the Holy Eucharist. The very sense of touch craved to feel the trickling waters of Baptism. The tongue was dry and the stomach empty with hunger to receive substantially the Bread of Life. Where, O Lord, cried out the bodily organs in unison, can we, even we, be united with Thee? In My Church, came the gracious reply, you will find Me indeed. There you will be united with Me as flesh of My flesh and bone of My bone, for the Church is My Body and the temple of My Spirit. Speaking to My son Paul after he had caused Stephen to be martyred, I told him that it was none other than I Whom he persecuted. When he was bound in chains for My sake, he sensed that he had in effect become a member of My Body, for he testified, "I live, yet not I, but Christ liveth in me."

From my most rudimentary notions of the Church, as I have outlined them here, it will be noted that I originally conceived of it as a visible and organic institution. The Protestant theory which reduced the Church to the status of a merely invisible society, consisting of the community of the elect, had no place in my thought. Such a society would not have answered the fundamental needs of which I have spoken and for which, I knew, Christ had made provision. The Church in which I was interested had certain organic functions, namely, to safeguard the integrity of the faith, to spread the Gospel to all nations, to enunciate the moral law, and to administer the Sacraments. None of the Protestant denominations even claimed to exercise all of these functions. They had reduced the number of the Sacraments from seven to two, or none. They denied the efficacy of the Sacraments, describing them as mere "signs" of election. None of these various sects, moreover, made any serious pretense to teach with finality the content of Christian dogma or of the moral law. For some of them faith was a word without content; others denied that faith was necessary at all. For many of these reformers Christ had, it seemed, suffered in vain the excruciating torments of his death. No debt of original sin, apparently, was thereby cancelled; no healing graces were thereby conferred.

If there existed any power on earth which could authoritatively declare what the Christian should believe and how he should act, and which could validly administer the Sacraments which Christ had instituted, there was no doubt in my mind that it was none of the Protestant sects. There was but one serious contender for the position, and that was the Catholic Church presided over by the Bishop of Rome.

Before admitting the claims of the Catholic Church, I exercised what I now regard as an excess of caution. I examined its credentials with all the diligence of which I was capable. I gave particular attention to the "notes" of the Church — those qualities which an institution fulfilling the Gospel promises must inevitably have: unicity ("that they may be one"), sanctity ("by this shall all men know that you are my disciples"), catholicity ("teaching all nations"), and apostolicity, which meant in effect historical identity with the original Church. All these qualities appeared to be present in the Roman Catholic communion as in no other.

I then asked myself whether the Catholic Church had exhibited infallibility ("He will teach you all things"). In order to answer this question I immersed myself in the intricacies of ecclesiastical history and delved into the complexities of medieval theology. I studied the decrees of numerous Councils from that of Nicaea to that of the Vatican, comparing them with modern Catholic catechisms. If I could find one inconsistency of dogma, one article of faith which the Church had been compelled to suppress or to retract, or one binding doctrine which was absurd in the light of reason or of natural science, I was resolved to conclude that there existed on earth no visible institution endowed with the powers which Christ had osten-

sibly vested in the Apostles. I read the most scath-
ing diatribes of Luther and of Calvin: I found
them eloquent but intemperate. Luther was
illogical and Calvin inhuman. I studied the controversies surrounding Galileo in the Seven-
teenth Century, and satisfied myself that the
Church had in no respect committed herself to
geocentrism. I studied the controversies surrounding Darwin in the Nineteenth Century, and
was astonished to discover that, even in the time
of Saint Thomas Aquinas, the Church had declared it possible that the human body had been
fashioned not instantaneously but by a series of
creative acts.

The more I examined, the more I was impressed with the consistency and sublimity of
Catholic doctrine. Through dark ages and enlightened, through ages of fervor and ages of corrup-
tion, under saintly popes and ordinary popes, the
treasure of the faith had been preserved intact.
Neither the sordid political issues at stake nor
the worldly cynicism of meddling statesmen had
been able to detract from the majestic decrees of
the Council of Trent. Not even the greed and
depravity of wicked pontiffs (of whom, be it
known, I found but few) had been capable of im-
pairing the integrity of Catholic doctrine. In peril
often, the deposit of the faith remained untar-
nished and entire. When Pope Sixtus V, that
energetic and high-minded reformer, had announced that he would publish and declare infallible his personal revision of the Vulgate,

containing several departures from the accepted text, Saint Robert Bellarmine had warned him, you will never live to see your new translation published. Ten years later, as the papal version of the Scriptures was being set up in the presses of Venice, Sixtus was taken ill and died. His successor laid the fresh parchments aside.[6]

Surely it was a divine protection which had saved the Church through all these centuries from the human failings of princes and prelates alike. Like the boat in which Christ slept, the Church was tossed by tempests, but was always safe. When one asked for an explanation, there could be but one reply: "Wist ye not that I was with you?"

Finally, I asked myself whether the Church had the appearances of being indefectible ("the gates of hell shall not prevail against it"). For nearly two thousand years, I noted, the voice of Holy Church had rung above the clamor of the nations. No fear of worldly opposition had silenced her, nor any desire to win applause seduced her. With uncompromising logic she continued to set forth the full content of the char-

---

6. [I believe I have here confused two separate incidents in the life of Bellarmine, one relating to Sixtus V's revised edition of the Vulgate and the other to the theological controversy about actual grace. Bellarmine regarded the unexpected death of Pope Sixtus before he issued his deficient verson of the Vulgate as providential; it convinced Bellarmine that if Clement VIII tried to condemn the opinion on grace that Bellarmine supported as orthodox, Providence would intervene to prevent the publication of the decree.]

ter of her liberties. The temporalities of the
Church were taken away, her jurisdiction over
spiritual matters abridged, and her claims of in-
direct political power repudiated by jealous secular rulers. In many lands she had been divested
of her teaching authority and her ecclesiastical
immunities were insolently violated. The great
powers of Europe, finding her yoke too harsh,
had many of them lapsed into heresy. Yet not
one claim did she retract. With patience and confidence amid calamities the successors of Peter
continued to admonish a deaf, unreasoning world.

Yet that voice still spoke and by many was
heeded. Empires had decayed, kingdoms had been
overthrown, philosophies outmoded, and heresies
forgotten. The strident voices of dictators rang
round the globe. The air was filled with the din
of wars and rumors of wars. Yet whither turned
the eyes of honest men, dismayed by the spectacle
of famine, slaughter, and appalling ruin? To
whom did their ears, pierced by the anguished
cries of the innocent, strain yet to listen? To the
pale occupant of Peter's chair in the beleaguered
Vatican.

Thither I turned also, to hear his voice, not
with the passing interest of the world, but with
that faith which, proving all things, holds fast to
that which is good.

Questioning could have been prolonged indefinitely. No saint or scholar is wise enough to
answer every possible doubt, or even every honest
difficulty. But I recognized that the essential had

been amply demonstrated and that the moment for action had come. I made an appointment to see a priest.

At the prearranged hour the doorbell of my apartment rang. Having been waiting alone, I went promptly to the door. A figure in black entered, tall, of modest demeanor, and slightly stooped – a scholar in appearance, yet not, I judged, a man lost in bookish abstractions. His face was frank and surprisingly human. What manner of man, I asked myself, stood before me? A madman who had thrown away his life in the practice of some strange and unlikely creed? Or was he a mysterious person chosen by God himself to perform on earth the supernatural work of Jesus Christ? I began my interrogation.

Brushing aside the social amenities, I proceeded directly to the point. The Catholic faith, I informed him, was very inviting but it unfortunately had a number of unpleasing and problematical features which would have to be cleared up without hesitation or ambiguity. At one moment, for example, Christ had said thus and so; at another moment He had said such and such. How did he, as a priest, propose to reconcile the apparent discrepancy?

My priest, however, was a busy man. He did not have time to waste in answering every hypothetical question which I was able to raise. He was interested, rather, in whether I was a good investment. After an hour's discussion, apparently satisfied that I had a fair acquaintance with the principles of Catholicism, he asked me almost impatiently what I had decided to do. I turned aside the question (deeming it a trifle unfair), and our meeting was soon ended.

For several days thereafter I did not see him. At last, however, I recognized that I had all the knowledge necessary to reach a decision. I met with him again and announced that I had determined to become a Catholic. He then instructed me painstakingly in the content of the Catholic faith in a series of thrilling conferences extending over a number of weeks. I was ready then, he said, to be received into the Church.

There were, of course, last minute doubts and hesitations. The very finality of the act appalled me. I would have been quite willing to make a profession of faith on a merely tentative basis. According to my best information at the present time, I would gladly have declared, it seems that there exist no reasonable grounds for doubt. But why, I objected, does God require me to commit myself for all my future days? I am young, and have much to learn. Already, in the span of a few years, I have changed my opinions many times, and things which once seemed obvious now seem false. The Mohammedans and the Buddhists believe and are in error. Does it not follow that I too, though certain, may yet be deceived? Certainty itself seemed insufficient. Desperately I asked myself how I could be certain that I would always remain certain.

In a sense, as I have said above, God does demand that we go beyond the evidence of reason. He declares, in effect, you must trust Me completely, that My word is the truth, and that I will not deceive you. Your childish waverings, He seemed to say, were based on the uncertainty of your own judgment. Now you must rely on Mine. The waters of faith look deep and dangerous before you enter them, but I give you My word that I will support and not betray you. You may stand all day if you please looking fearfully down at the water. I will not force you to move; but by standing where you are you will not get any nearer nor will the leap become any easier.

I came into the Church like one of those timid swimmers who closes his eyes as he jumps into the roaring sea. The waters of faith, I have since found, are marvelously buoyant. Indeed, when man is clothed with grace, the sea of faith is his natural element.

I felt, in addition, a natural reluctance to take any action which would estrange me from my family and friends. The call of Christ must be obeyed, but I would gladly have dispensed with the religious cleavage. After becoming a Catholic, it appeared, I could no longer be at ease with persons divided from me by so wide a chasm.

This difficulty, like the other, dissolved as soon as I had pronounced the baptismal vows. I immediately acquired new and exquisite friendships based on a common seeking for the things of God. Nor were the old ties broken off or weakened. Through the love of Christ, I found myself drawn closer to the entire human family. They, on the other hand, did not turn away from me because of my conversion. Among my family and friends I found very little hostility to the Catholic religion. Most of them were interested, with an interest born of human affection, to learn the motives which had prompted me to enter the Church. It is in part for them that I write these pages, hoping to account for my actions more fully here than I have been able to do previously.

My first sensation after receiving the conditional baptism which the Church confers on nearly all her Protestant converts was one of freedom. Very little in this respect had been sacrificed. I had renounced only that which I firmly recognized as error. A tremendous amount, on the other hand, had been gained. Here was liberty to believe and accept and love with all one's heart without any misgiving or restraint. Here was unlimited access to the wonderful gifts which Christ had lavished on His chosen Spouse, the Church. As a member incorporated in Christ's Mystical Body (for Our Lord and His Spouse are but one flesh), I could participate fully in the liturgical life of the Church on earth. And not on earth only I was also united with the Church Suffering in Purgatory and with the Church Triumphant, where the saints rejoice in heaven. I was intimately associated with the holy souls in Purgatory, whom I could benefit by my prayers, and with the saints in heaven, from whose superabundant merits I could freely draw. They, whose works and writings I had so much admired from afar, now became all mine. My saints, I could call upon them at will and receive their personal attention. It was as though they had lived and labored but for me.

Having become a Catholic, I was surprised to discover that my conversion had scarcely begun. I had previously imagined that I would instantly embark upon a heroic course of action. I had imagined that I would not share the weakness and timidity which made the Catholic men and women of my acquaintance act so much like their non-Catholic neighbors. In this I was wrong, totally wrong. One's human nature remains, and with it all the tendencies of pride and selfishness which faith condemns. I find myself, as a Catholic, incapable of living without compromise according to my beliefs. Indeed my faith, strong as it is, has penetrated only a small portion of my mind. Many of my opinions, imbibed from an unbelieving world, are inconsistent with my religious convictions. My natural sentiments are almost completely unbaptized. When I am insulted, anger and indignation rise within me as strongly as they did before. When delayed, I am impatient. When treated unjustly, I revile and do not bless. The most ordinary works of mercy, such as giving to the poor, visiting the sick, and counseling the doubtful, are irksome to me. If I do them at all, it is in a half-hearted and ungenerous spirit which renders them practically worthless. Any heathen with a spark of natural goodness can put me to shame in matters of tact and human warmth. When it comes to the most elemental acts of public devotion, I am so embarrassed to appear different from others that it is a painful effort even to bless myself at meals.

Does that mean that my faith is void and unprofitable? Far from it. Brethren outside the Church, do not be scandalized by the frailty and ineptitude of Catholics. Our human faults, the whole burden of fallen nature, remain with us as much as with you. Your conduct is often more praiseworthy than ours. The sufficiency of which we seem to boast so much lies not in ourselves, but in Christ. There is no sin so hideous that He refuses to pay the debt for it, provided that we go to Him with sorrow, humble love, and confidence.

The acquisition of virtuous tendencies is a slow and difficult process, in which many of us will never greatly succeed. By the power of our own will we can to some extent avoid the more conspicuous acts of sin. But the evil, thus repressed, continues to live underground, and, unless grace be present, will exhibit itself in other ways such as the stiff-necked complacency of the Pharisees. The world will never condemn secret pride as bitterly as it condemns the shameful sins. But Christ condemned it more severely because it is more incompatible with love.

True progress can be made through love alone. By forgetting ourselves and living entirely for the glory of Almighty God we can unite ourselves efficaciously with Jesus Christ, Who offered His Sacred Humanity to the Father without stint or hesitation. When one lives completely in the presence of God and for His sake, commendable actions become easier and more fruitful. The saints are able to conform their actions fully with their faith, exercising the necessary tact and delicacy, because they possess the crowning virtue of simplicity. Their whole body is filled with light because their eye is single. They have acquired the spirit of prayer.

In the Catholic life, outward manifestations are always secondary to interior virtues. Even the most dramatic feats of heroism avail nothing if the spirit be lacking. The merit of Saint Francis consisted not in exchanging his knightly attire for a beggar's rags, but in being able to live a life of poverty and want with unceasing joy and gratitude. He loved God so much that he was incapable of becoming discouraged or embittered, even for an instant, in adversity.

As the past recedes into obscurity, I watch it disappear without nostalgia. I recall it with difficulty and without delight. The man who looks toward Christ looks always forward, striving constantly to become more worthy of his divine Lover, hoping to draw a little closer to Him in this world and, after a little while, to be united with Him in everlastingness.

To advance in the life of grace is to become more childlike, more conscious of one's own littleness and ineffectiveness and of the bigness and strength of God. Gradually, and after many falls, we learn how to cast all our care on Him Who has a fatherly care for us, to trust Him completely because He is all-wise, all-loving, and all-powerful. As one loses oneself in Him one learns what it is to wrestle against principalities and powers. At the same time, however, one learns the meaning of that peace which was the parting gift of Christ to His children in the world.

Through a gradual growth in humble Christian hope and faith and love one rises on the ladder of perfection. The ascent is difficult because the spiritual life is a continual struggle. The field to be subdued is as broad as the eye can see, and as one rises the horizons widen. Yet the struggle is not without rich rewards, even at the bottom rungs of the ladder.

Reflections on a
Theological Journey

# Reflections on a Theological Journey

I. The War Years

In a sense I could say, as did John Henry Newman in his *Apologia pro vita sua,* that there is no further history of my religious opinions, since in becoming a Catholic I arrived at my real home. My views regarding God, Christ, and the Church have not substantially changed, but I have filled out with theological reflection what was previously a basic stance of faith. Although my faith-journey was complete, my theological journeyings were just beginning. In updating the story, I have thought it might be appropriate to say something about my theological pilgrimage since 1940.

The war years were for me a time of growing into my new faith. As I moved from ship to ship and from shore base to shore base I was fortunate in meeting fellow Catholics and chaplains who sustained my faith. When stationed at Naples toward the end of the European war, I lived ashore, assisted at daily Mass at a parish church, and had two memorable trips to Rome, where I was able to attend audiences with Pope Pius XII. I looked up to this pope as a faithful bearer of the Petrine office in troubled times, and with the passage of years I came to appreciate his teaching on biblical studies, on the Church as mystical Body, on the liturgy, and on the active participation of the laity in the life of the Church. Through initiatives such as these, combined with his teaching on war and peace, he helped to prepare the ground for the Second Vatican Council.

In the spring of 1946, as I was being released from active duty, I lived for several months in Cambridge, Massachusetts, where I was able to spend most of my time at St. Benedict Center. This was a thriving Catholic student center located in close proximity to Harvard University. In the spring of 1941 I had been one of its three founders. In the intervening years, while I was absent in naval service, the Center had risen to new heights of vitality under the inspiring leadership of Catherine Goddard Clarke, a remarkable woman who had been my godmother at my reception into the Church. During my absence she had obtained the services of Father Leonard Feeney, an extraordinarily talented Jesuit, who made the Center his principal apostolate. Father Feeney was a poet, an actor, and a public speaker on fire with contagious devotion to the faith and apostolic zeal.[1] One of Father Feeney's devotions that especially appealed to me was to the Doctors of the Church, twenty-nine outstanding theologians officially recognized for their sanctity and orthodoxy, who had defended and developed

---

1. For some impressions and recollections see my "Leonard Feeney: In Memoriam," *America* 138 (February 25, 1978): 135-37.

Catholic teaching in different crises. (The number of the Doctors has since risen to 32.) With the intention of writing a book on the Doctors, I drafted the first three chapters, on Athanasius, Hilary, and Ephrem. The chapter on Ephrem was published in the second issue of *From the House-tops,* a quarterly that I helped to launch in my last days at the Center.

A few years after my departure, St. Benedict Center became involved in a bitter controversy about the question of salvation outside the Catholic Church. The rigid positions attributed to Father Feeney and his disciples were not a part of my experience, though I did observe, and support, his efforts to confront non-Catholics with the full challenge of the faith. After a period under interdict, Father Feeney and most of his followers were restored to full communion with the Church. In its new location at Still River, Massachusetts, the Center was transformed into a Benedictine priory and in 1993, some fifteen years after Father Feeney's death, was raised to the status of an abbey. I was able to be present for the installation of Gabriel Gibbs as the first abbot. Meanwhile, a number of the women associated with the Center formed a separate community, St. Scholastica Priory at Petersham, Massachusetts, where they continue to carry on a fruitful apostolate of prayer and worship. Two choirs, one of monks and the other of nuns, exquisitely sing the liturgy in the old Gregorian plainchant.

II. Jesuit Training

As soon as my discharge from the Navy was complete, I was in a position to fulfill an ambition I had had since my first days as a Catholic by joining the Society of Jesus. In August 1946 I entered St. Andrew-on-Hudson, the novitiate of the New York Province, a large and rather austere edifice beautifully situated on a hill overlooking the Hudson River near Poughkeepsie. It was an ideal spot for induction into the religious life. The novices were a varied group. Some were college graduates just emerging from service in the armed forces, but the majority were bright young men just out of high school. We all lived by a strict rule of silence, with only short periods of recreation, and spent several hours a day on our knees in prayer. When novices had to speak outside of times of recreation, the mandatory language was Latin, the official language of the Society and of the Church. Their reading was restricted to Holy Scripture, Jesuit history, lives of saints, and ascetical theology. Newspapers, radio, and television were out of the question.

I felt enormously privileged to be able to spend two years of my life concentrating on the figure of Jesus Christ as Savior and Lord. I grew to love the Spiritual Exercises of St. Ignatius of Loyola, which solidified my sense of being called to labor as a companion of Jesus in extending the Kingdom of Christ and building up the Church. The Ignatian Rules for the Discernment of Spirits and for Thinking with the Church seemed to me to epitomize the mystical and ecclesial dimensions of the Jesuit vocation. Applied in the context of contemplations of the life of Christ, these sets of rules give the key to the Ignatian method of decision-making. As a theologian, I have found the Ignatian rules applicable to the process by which individual theologians, and the Church in its corporate actions, reach decisions about matters of doctrine.

After completing my novitiate, I spent three years studying philosophy at the Jesuit scholasticate in Woodstock, Maryland. The faculty had recently abandoned Suarezianism for a purer version of Thomism, based primarily on the original texts of Aquinas. Considerable reference was made to contemporary Thomistic philosophers such as Étienne Gibson and Jacques Maritain, both of whom I had come to admire as an undergraduate at Harvard. When I arrived at Woodstock, I asked the dean for his advice on what I should be reading in my spare time. He told me that most Catholics know St. Thomas chiefly from his two great Summas (the *Summa theologia* and the *Summa contra Gentiles*), and that I would do well to study some of the earlier works in which many of the same questions were treated in greater detail. Following his recommendation, I began by reading with great relish the *De veritate*. I was deeply impressed by the emphasis that St. Thomas placed on the eternal Logos as the exemplary prototype of creation. After completing the *De veritate,* I spent my remaining leisure time reading Thomas' great commentary on the

Sentences of Peter Lombard. In studying this I was especially struck by the magnificent phenomenology of love in the third book (Distinctions 27-30). After reading passages such as this, I could never be convinced that St. Thomas was dry and abstract, or remote from experience. The scholastic format of his writings often conceals the living personality of the author.

For me the study of philosophy was a delightful exercise in contemplation. I have always had an avidity for viewing things in their total context. Philosophy expanded my vision by presenting a view of the whole of reality, both created and uncreated. With the help of authors such as Thomas Aquinas, I came to look on God as the only self-explanatory being, the sole entity whose existence was not problematic. I was impressed by the existential fragility and questionableness of everything that is not God. For me philosophy was an aid to the spiritual life. It enhanced my sense of dependence on God, and of gratitude to him for all that was beautiful and good.

In the next two years of my Jesuit career, from 1951 to 1953, I was assigned to teach philosophy at Fordham University in New York. I tried to pass on to my students the type of modern Thomism in which I had been trained at Woodstock.[2] During these years I found myself busily

---

2. For the type of philosophy that I and other Jesuits of the day were teaching, see *Introductory Metaphysics,* by Avery Dulles, James Demske, and Robert O'Connell (New York: Sheed & Ward, 1955).

occupied not only with teaching but with student activities, especially in moderating the Sodality of the Blessed Virgin. The students who joined this organization were remarkably serious about their faith and spiritual life. They followed a strict regime that included daily Mass, examination of conscience, meditation, and works of charity. I was also involved in setting up at Fordham a chapter of the Catholic Evidence Guild – a project in which we received helpful guidance from the publisher Frank Sheed.

During this period of regency I got to know something of the Catholic life of New York City, speaking at various clubs and centers. I frequently attended meetings of the Oriel Society, a group of eager Catholic intellectuals, some of them recent converts to the faith. This society met at the mid-town residence of an apostolically minded layman, Maurice Leahy. The summer schools at Fordham were an exciting time, enlivened by the presence on campus of distinguished visiting professors, including Jesuits such as Paul Henry and Gustave Weigel. The theology courses that I audited whetted my appetite to begin formal studies in that field.

In 1953 I returned to Woodstock as a convinced Thomist, eager to study theology. Under the guidance of Father Gustave Weigel I developed a special interest in the act of faith and in ecclesiology, two treatises that he taught. At my request Father Weigel guided me in much of my private reading. After taking me through the entire corpus of Cyprian, he introduced me to the study of the ecumenical movement, in which Catholics were just beginning to get involved. The World Council of Churches was at the time preparing for its Second Assembly, to be held at Evanston in 1954. Father Weigel also familiarized me with the work of Paul Tillich, whom he regarded as the most brilliant theologian on the American scene. From Tillich I first learned the importance of symbol for the theology of revelation.

Interesting though I found these ecumenical ventures, my heart was more drawn to the *nouvelle théologie* which had begun to develop in France at the close of World War II. I tried to read as much as I could of authors such as Henri de Lubac, Jean Daniélou, and Yves Congar, all of whom were retrieving the patristic and medieval heritage in a modern context. The program of *ressourcement,* magnificently exemplified by these theologians, prepared me for the developments that would before long overtake the Church, with John XXIII and the Second Vatican Council.

After my ordination to the priesthood in 1956, and an additional year of study at Woodstock, I was sent to Germany, where I completed at Münster a final year of pastoral and spiritual formation known as "tertianship" (a "third year" of novitiate). Besides immersing myself in Jesuit lore and in the Catholic tradition of prayer and mysticism, I took advantage of the opportunity

to acquaint myself with the progress of ecumenism in Western Europe. During the summers of
1957 and 1958 I visited ecumenical centers in
Paris, Amsterdam, Berlin, Heidelberg, Mainz,
and Niederaltaich, and became acquainted with
some of the leading figures in that field, both
Lutheran and Catholic. The following year, 1959,
I attended a fascinating meeting of the Conference on Ecumenical Questions at Paderborn.
Bishop Lorenz Jaeger, Monsignor Jan Wille-
brands, and Fathers Yves Congar, C.J. Dumont,
Bernard Leeming, and Hans Küng, among others,
formulated and discussed proposals for the ecumenical agenda of the forthcoming council, which
had just been announced by Pope John XXIII.
Many of the suggestions formulated at this meeting, after passing through the Papal Secretariat
for Promoting Christian Unity, found their way
into Vatican II's Decree on Ecumenism.

When I arrived at Rome in the fall of 1958
for doctoral studies at the Pontifical Gregorian
University, my interests were divided between
medieval Scholasticism and contemporary ecumenism. I submitted to Bernard Lonergan a thesis proposal on the metaphor of "illumination" in
the religious epistemology of St. Thomas. He told
me he would think about the feasibility of the
project, but by the time he sent me his note of
approval I had already signed up with Father
Jan Witte, a Dutch expert on ecumenism, to work
on the subject of *vestigia ecclesiae,* the "traces of
the Church" ostensibly found outside the true

Church of Christ. In the course of writing the dissertation I narrowed down the topic to deal only with the participation of Protestant churches in the prophetic office of the one Church of Christ. The conclusions of my thesis, rather laboriously worked out, seemed bold at the time, but five years later, in the light of Vatican II's Decree on Ecumenism, they had become common Catholic doctrine. I am glad that I did not publish the dissertation, because it was rapidly outstripped by developments in current history.

Before returning to the United States I made several stops in Germany, Austria, Switzerland, and France. A high point was my visit to the Protestant monastery at Taizé, near Cluny, where the prior, Roger Schutz, impressed me as a deeply spiritual leader. I had some fine conversations there with the theologian Max Thurian, whose work was later to be so vital for the Faith and Order document on Baptism, Eucharist, and Ministry. Thurian has subsequently become a Catholic and a priest of the archdiocese of Naples, but he continues his scholarly work at Taizé and Geneva. When I was appointed to the International Theological Commission in 1992, I was delighted to find that he had also been made a member. It has been a pleasure to collaborate with him on that commission.

III. Teaching at Woodstock

In the spring of 1960, as I was completing my doctoral studies in Rome, I received a letter from my provincial superior in New York that I was to teach theology at Woodstock. My assignment, beginning the next September, was to take over the courses on apologetics, revelation, and biblical inspiration that had been taught by Father Vincent O'Keefe, who was being transferred to Fordham. During the summer I struggled to acquire some competence in the new directions of biblical studies, which were vitally important, especially for apologetics. I found that tools such as source criticism, form criticism, and redaction criticism, moderately used, could be helpful for understanding and appreciating the Gospels. With the assistance of some materials left behind by Father O'Keefe and some notes composed by René Latourelle, a Canadian Jesuit teaching at the Gregorian, I was able to piece together a course on revelation very much along the lines of what would become official Catholic doctrine with Vatican II's Constitution on Divine Revelation.

As for my course on inspiration, I had already been attracted by Pierre Benoit's retrieval of St. Thomas' doctrine on prophecy as a resource for constructing a doctrine of biblical inspiration. Benoit's theory of inspiration as an illumination of the author's practical judgment seemed to me to avoid some of the pitfalls of earlier theories, especially with respect to inerrancy. At the same time I was drawn by the theory of Karl Rahner, which connected biblical inspiration with God's historical action in the foundation of the Church. Rahner convinced me that the Scriptures were a constitutive element of the early Church, expressing its faith in a "canonical" form that could be normative for posterity. I tried to build this idea into my own teaching on the inspiration of Scripture.

In July 1961 I delivered five lectures on apologetics at a summer institute on Scripture, summarizing some of the fruits of my first year of teaching. When I published these lectures under the title *Apologetics and the Biblical Christ,*[3] they attracted considerable attention because of their critique of the prevalent approach through scientific history. My main point was that apologetics could not be content to rely on academic historical method and but that it must build rather on the power of committed religious testimony.

Because the Bible is essentially a testimony to the faith of the authors and of the communities in which it was composed, rather than a work of dispassionate factual history, it lends itself to this apologetic approach. In recent years I have had several occasions to reiterate my views on apologetics and testimony in the context of contemporary efforts to revive the "quest of the historical Jesus."

The major theological event of the early 1960s was the Second Vatican Council. Gustave Weigel and John Courtney Murray, two of Woodstock's faculty members, served as *periti* and kept our community well informed of the dramatic debates

---

3. Avery Dulles, *Apologetics and the Biblical Christ,* Woodstock Paper No. 6 (Westminster, MD: Newman, 1963).

concerning the Dogmatic Constitution on Divine
Revelation, the Decree on Ecumenism, the Declaration on the Jews (eventually incorporated in
the Declaration on Non-Christian Religions), the
Declaration on Religious Freedom, and the Dogmatic Constitution on the Church.

Together with practically everyone at Woodstock, I applauded the achievements of the Council, including its openness to the values of
modernity, dialogue, and personal freedom. But
I felt it necessary to combine these attitudes with
my continued allegiance to Thomas Aquinas, Ignatius of Loyola and, in general, the great medieval and baroque heritage of music, art,
literature, philosophy, and theology. While many
of the conciliar and postconciliar reforms were
no doubt prudent and necessary accommodations
to the times, they did not all strike me as im-
provements. It was difficult for me to accept the
virtual banishment of Latin from the liturgy and
the substitution of new popular tunes for the
imposing Gregorian chant or the mellifluous Renaissance polyphony. The depreciation of devotion
to the saints and the removal of shrines and stat-
ues from the churches stuck me as impoverish-
ments that had to be regretfully endured. It might
be necessary, I concluded, to live through a barren
season of slovenly improvisation until the Church
could experience some kind of cultural revival.

After the untimely death of Father Weigel in
January 1964, Father Murray commissioned me,
as it were, to become an interpreter of the Council

for the benefit of Catholics in the United States, a task that I gladly took upon myself for the remainder of the decade. I felt it necessary to show why the changes introduced by the Council were justified, but at the same time to caution against the tendency to carry the spirit of the Council far beyond the letter, and to portray Catholic polity and dogma as if they were subject to perpetual reinvention.

In the late 1960s, seeking to make a strong case for the new directions set by Vatican II, I may have tended to exaggerate the novelty of the Council's doctrine and the shortcomings of the preconciliar period. But after 1970, as the Catholic left became more strident, and as young Catholics began to dismiss or ignore the heritage of previous centuries, I felt it necessary to put greater emphasis on continuity with the past. As so often, the error was that of fixing on partial or transitory elements and failing to see the picture as a whole. No one segment of history or cultural perspective can be taken as embodying the totality of Catholic truth, as if it were a norm by which all other ages and cultures could be judged. The reigning tendency to identify the good with the fruits of contemporary Western democratic culture struck me as particularly questionable.

The middle sixties were a difficult period. Some of the students, imbued with the youth culture of the "new breed" were convinced that no one over thirty could have anything of interest to say. Seminaries were rocked by the impact of radical secularization, the "God-is-dead" theology, the S.D.S. (Students for a Democratic Society), and violent protests against the Vietnam War. The agitation came to a climax after 1968, the year of the assassinations of Robert Kennedy and Martin Luther King, the riots in the universities and inner cities, and, in the Catholic Church, the vehement reactions to Paul VI's encyclical on birth control, *Humanae vitae.*

Practically all my theological colleagues were convinced that the pope had erred in rejecting the majority report of his own commission, and I was under some pressure to sign statements to that effect. Not being a moral theologian, I did not feel competent to pronounce on the intrinsic arguments put forth by both sides. Having been trained to believe exactly what the pope was now teaching, I had no personal reasons for dissent, and I considered that the burden of proof must be borne by those who wanted the doctrine changed. I saw no reason why the pope, with his special charisms of office, should be obliged to follow the majority of a purely advisory commission. But I also thought, and declared, that since the pope had not invoked his power to teach infallibly, Catholics who conscientiously dissented were not to be treated as if they had renounced the faith. For this reason I was often regarded as a dissenter myself, although I never personally opposed the pope's teaching nor did I affix my name to any dissenting declaration. With the passage of years I came to appreciate the prophetic significance of *Humanae vitae,* in which the consequences of the new sexual revolution were accurately predicted.

The controversy about *Humanae vitae* dispelled certain naïve expectations regarding the "preestablished harmony" between the pope and other elements in the Church, namely the bishops, the laity, and the theologians. By reacting in different ways to *Humanae vitae,* the national and regional conferences of bishops undermined some of the teaching authority that had been attributed to them since Vatican II. Their diverse interpretations could not all be right. While the conferences undoubtedly served a useful purpose in the pastoral mediation of doctrine, they were not independent doctrinal authorities. Whatever doctrinal authority they possessed accrued to them from their communion with the episcopacy as a whole and with the pope as the head of the episcopal college.

As dissent from *Humanae vitae* was hailed and promoted by the press and other media, many of the laity became confused about what to believe. Some were persuaded that to accept the papal teaching would be to forfeit the freedom of conscience that had been won for them at Vatican II. A sounder interpretation of the Council made it evident that Catholic freedom of conscience does not exist without the corresponding obligation to form one's conscience in the light of Church teaching. The "sense of the faithful" could not serve as a theological source unless the faithful in question were motivated by an ecclesial spirit, and thus reflected the "sense of the Church."

IV. Contestation and Mediation

The years following *Humanae vitae* were a period of lively ferment in which Catholics were reconsidering practically everything in their heritage. In the hope of achieving some measure of consensus, committees and advisory councils were set up in great numbers. Like others, I spent vast amounts of time serving on committees dealing with academic curriculum, Jesuit life, Catholic doctrine, and ecumenical relations.

Among the more interesting of these assignments was the United States Bishops' National Advisory Council, initially established in 1969 as the Advisory Council to the United States Catholic Conference. It was a group of fifty appointed persons, predominantly from the laity, but including a small number of bishops, priests, and religious. Selected for diversity as well as competence, this group was like a microcosm of the Church in this country, except that the representatives were uncommonly articulate. Beginning in 1969, the semiannual meetings of this group gave advisory opinions on all major items coming up before the meetings of the United States bishops. In the first years the Advisory Council devoted much attention to items such as the Black Manifesto and the concerns of Hispanic Catholics. It also made a considerable contribution to the launching of the Campaign for Human Development. Much of our energy was taken up with plans for a National Pastoral Council, according to a proposal that originated, I believe, with Archbishop (later Cardinal) John Dearden. Although we tried to publicize the idea through literature and public consultations, the proposal of a National Pastoral Council did not seem to arouse much enthusiasm at the grass roots level. Meanwhile, as a result of pastoral councils such as that held in Holland, Rome began to express its misgivings about such assemblies. The bishops at length concluded that the project was not for the present advisable.

The proximity of the bicentennial of the United States Declaration of Independence in 1976 suggested to members of the Advisory Council a somewhat different agenda. Plans were already being laid for a Eucharistic Congress at Philadelphia, which would give an opportunity to celebrate the achievements of the ecumenical dialogues of the previous decade regarding the Eucharist. Could not this ecclesial event be paralleled by another, dealing with Church-world relations? The American bishops, acting on this proposal from the Advisory Council, decided to sponsor a program of "Liberty and Justice for All."

The Eucharistic Congress was a great success, as was the accompanying ecumenical workshop. Members of different dialogue groups discussed the advances that had been made. For instance, George Lindbeck and I teamed up to discuss the Lutheran-Catholic convergences on Eucharist doctrine, and we had a large and eager audience including Mother Teresa of Calcutta, who was brought to this relatively tranquil theological event to shield her from the mob of her admirers.

The bishops' program of "Liberty and Justice for All" was boldly conceived. It began with the collection of more than 800,000 individual responses from parishioners to determine the concerns and attitudes of grassroots Catholics. These questionnaires were supplemented by a series of meetings, including seven regional "justice hearings" at which prominent members of the clergy and laity presented testimony. I was asked to make the initial presentation at the first hearing in Washington, D.C., in February 1975, on the social mission of the Church. Eight committees were then constituted to compose working papers that would draw on the questionnaires and the hearings, so as to set forth programs for the future. I served on the committee dealing with "Church." These "white papers," as they came to be called, were then used as a draft for the resolutions of a national Catholic assembly, called the "Call to Action" conference, which met at Detroit in October 1976.

The assembly at Detroit was nothing if not dramatic. More than 100 bishops were in attendance. A total of 1340 delegates came from 150 dioceses and 94 national Catholic organizations as varied as the Catholic Committee for Urban Ministry, Network, the Center of Concern, the Quixote Center, and a variety of questionably Catholic organizations representing gay and lesbian activists, resigned priests, and the like. In three short days, the carefully nuanced working papers were gutted by a series of radical amendments, resulting in some 182 resolutions, including some that called for ordination of women, acceptance of married priests, the admission of divorced and remarried Catholics to the sacraments, freedom of conscience regarding contraception, amnesty to those who had evaded military service, condemnation of the production and threat to use nuclear weapons, support for the Equal Rights Amendment, and the end of all discrimination against homosexuals. Many of these resolutions could not be accepted by the bishops, either because they were contrary to Catholic doctrine or because they were beyond the competence of the national conference.

The Call to Action assembly provided an object lesson in how a small group of militant activists could manipulate a large majority of open-minded liberal delegates, thus aligning the assembly with an agenda that had little in common with the Catholic tradition, the social teaching of the Church, and the concerns of the great majority of worshipers. The process exhibited the naïveté of the organizers and led to a defeat of the intentions of the bishops who had hoped to usher in a new era of coresponsibility and participation in the life and government of the Church in this nation. What eventuated was a polarized situation that pitted reformers against conservatives. To this day the "Call to Action" movement continues to press for the adoption of the rejected proposals of the Detroit meeting and thus gives a voice to groups that would like to see a Catholic Church organized along liberal democratic lines.

My own concerns during the tumultuous decade following Vatican II were theological rather than social or pastoral. Difficult questions were raised by the widespread dissent within the theological community. Did the theologians have any teaching authority, or was the hierarchical magisterium the only teaching organ in the Church? What was the binding force of papal teaching when it did not claim to be passing on revealed doctrine or when it did not claim to be speaking with infallibility? Issues such as these were high on the theological agenda of the period after *Humanae vitae,* and I attempted to grapple with them in a series of books and articles.[4]

The most commercially successful of my books from this period was *Models of the Church,* published in 1974.[5] It was intended not as a systematic ecclesiology but as a prolegomenon, lay-

---

4. See, for instance, the articles published in *The Survival of Dogma* (1971), *The Resilient Church* (1977), *A Church to Believe In* (1982), and *The Reshaping of Catholicism* (1988).

5. Avery Dulles, *Models of the Church* (Garden City, NY: Doubleday, 1974). An expanded edition, still in print, was published by Doubleday Image, New York, in 1987.

ing out the dominant schools of thought under the rubric of models. Whereas the neo-scholastic methodology of the recent past would have favored a clear option in favor of a single image or concept, and the branding of all the others as false, I preferred a more dialogic approach. Father Weigel had convinced me that the Church as a mystery could not be contained under any conceptual definition. Rather, it should be designated by a variety of images and metaphors, each of which captured certain limited aspects of the complex reality. A selective use of such figures, I believed, underlay the divisions between opposed theological schools, none of which had the total truth, and none of which was totally wrong.

Some people read my *Models* book as though I were encouraging the reader to make a choice among the models, but my intention was rather the opposite. I wanted to make people aware of the unspoken assumptions that underlay their own options and to open them up to dialogue with Catholics who operated on different assumptions. Because all five models, as I tried to show, had both strengths and weaknesses, it would be a mistake to opt exclusively for any one. If it were necessary to make a choice, I would have selected the sacramental model, which seemed to have the greatest potentiality for integrating within itself the strong points of the other four models.

In subsequent works on revelation and faith I continued to use the "method of models" set forth in *Models of the Church*. I consider that, since revelation is carried by Scripture and living tradition, and since faith comes through hearing, the theologian must begin by listening to what the source-documents and the faithful of the past have said. After having assimilated the theological tradition by a survey of the history, the theologian should attempt to find the points of agreement and disagreement among reflective believers. The models, as ways of systematizing characteristic positions or schools of thought, make it possible to survey the ground. Where there are differences between schools, the theologian should try to construct a synthesis, saving the valid insights of the various thinkers, perhaps by incorporating them into a new paradigm. In my theological explorations I have attempted to retrieve what is best in the tradition, to reject one-sided opinions, and contribute to the formation of a fruitful consensus. This task seems to me to be particularly urgent in view of the confusing proliferation of dubious new opinions with which the market is currently being flooded.

V. Years in Washington

Several changes in my professional career occurred during the decade of the 1970s. In 1969 Woodstock College moved to temporary quarters in New York City, and in 1973 it began to be phased out, as a result of a decision by the American provincial superiors to reduce the number of theologates. The New York and Maryland Provinces then inaugurated the Woodstock Theological Center in

Washington, D.C., and I was asked to take a role in its establishment. In this new incarnation Woodstock has sought to provide an example of how theology could be done in a nonacademic setting, dealing with problems that can be handled less successfully in seminaries and in graduate schools. The Woodstock Theological Center has concerned itself predominantly with problems of social justice and business ethics and with the moral responsibilities of persons in government. The presence of this institution in the nation's capital, in affiliation with Georgetown University, has been a blessing. Although the Woodstock Center has never been my primary apostolate, my association with it has helped me to work with a broader horizon, avoiding confinement either within the seminary or within the academy.[6]

When I moved to Washington in 1974 I also accepted a professorship at The Catholic University of America, where I continued to teach for the next fourteen years. With the older generation of theologians dying off (Murray himself had died in 1967), I found myself thrust increasingly into positions of leadership. I took on the presidency of the Catholic Theological Society of America in 1975-1976, and the presidency of the American

---

6. In my address on the occasion of the twentieth anniversary of the Woodstock Theological Center, I had an occasion to emphasize the Ignatian inspiration of the kind of theological reflection sponsored by the Center – the methodology of apostolic discernment accompanied by serious prayer. See my "Appreciation and Challenge," *Woodstock Report* 39 (October 1994): 8-9.

Theological Society in 1978-1979. I was also asked to serve as a consultant for various committees of the National Conference of Catholic Bishops, especially in the areas of doctrine and ecumenism. Believing as I do in the essentially ecclesial character of theology, I have always tried to make myself available to the hierarchical leadership when it has sought assistance from theologians.

Since 1971 I have devoted a great deal of time to the United States Lutheran-Catholic Dialogue. This group was especially productive in the mid-1970s, when theologians of the stature of Walter Burghardt, Raymond Brown, Arthur Carl Piepkorn, and Warren Quanbeck, all of whom had been with the dialogue from its early days, were still contributing their services. I learned a great deal from the Lutheran participants, who were excellent scholars well versed in their own confessional heritage. Their questions to Catholics forced me to think about subjects that I had previously neglected and to nuance a number of my ideas on subjects familiar to me.

The statements of this dialogue on Papal Primacy, on Teaching Authority and Infallibility, and on Justification were significant ecumenical breakthroughs, removing various obstacles that stood in the way of ecclesial reconciliation. The very success of these statements raised difficult questions about the reasons why Lutherans and Catholics had to belong to different churches. Some Lutherans and Catholics seem to feel it incumbent on them to discover grave doctrinal differences in order to justify the existing ecclesial separation. While this defensiveness should be resisted, it is also necessary to be on guard against the excesses of ecumenical enthuasiasts. It would be unrealistic to speak as though virtually complete agreement between Lutherans and Catholics had been reached, rendering the remaining differences unimportant.

From my experience in interconfessional conversations, I have been impressed by the value and limitations of dialogue. Dialogue can present a temptation to downplay the differences for the sake of reporting an apparent consensus, but this does not seem to be the only, or the dominant, risk. More often, I think, the parties become strengthened in their confessional consciousness. An effort is required to overcome inherited stereotypes concerning the other party and to find the common convictions that frequently underlie the different formulations used by each side. But there are limits to dialogue. Not infrequently it discloses hard-core differences that cannot be overcome except through conversion. On a number of points our Lutheran-Catholic dialogue came across divergences that, to all appearances, cannot be resolved by dialogue alone.[7]

---

7. Such divergences were already recognized in the early stages of the dialogue, but were not emphasized. They came more into the open in later volumes such as *The One Mediator, the Saints, and Mary* (1992) and *Scripture and Tradition* (1995). All nine volumes of the *Lutherans and Catholics in Dialogue* are available through the Augsburg Press, Minneapolis.

One of the high points of my ecumenical experience was the Faith and Order Conference at Lima, Peru, early in 1982. I was invited by the American Lutheran William H. Lazareth, the Director of the Faith and Order Commission of the World Council of Churches. Professor Geoffrey Wainwright, presiding over the committee dealing with Baptism, Eucharist, and Ministry, asked me to serve as secretary of his committee. My task was to commit to writing the final text that would be transmitted to the whole commission for a vote. I had to type it on a borrowed Spanish-language typewriter with all sorts of tildes and inverted question marks on keys where I would have expected something else. Notwithstanding all physical impediments, the text was completed and received unanimous approval in the general session. It was a carefully crafted piece of work – the culmination, one might say, of fifty years of Faith and Order discussions. Yet it was not a full consensus. Disputed points were indicated in the Commission's commentary, which was printed as an integral part of the document because it is essential for the correct interpretation of the convergences in the main text.

The aftermath of *Humanae vitae* continued to be troublesome throughout the 1970s and beyond. During my presidency of the CTSA a committee on human sexuality, established by a previous president, submitted a report that contested the official Catholic teaching on many issues. Like several other members of the Board of Directors, I was dissatisfied with the report, but we had to admit that the committee had fulfilled its mandate, which was to submit its own conclusions.

The Board eventually worked out a compromise, to the effect that the report would be "received" (not "accepted" or "approved"), that the CTSA would not publish the report under its own auspices, and that the authors would not publish it until they had read and responded to the comments of several moral theologians, which they agreed to take seriously as a basis for possible revisions. Some excellent critiques were produced and submitted to the authors, but they did not make significant changes before they published the report on their own authority the following year.

In the 1980s a new crisis occurred in connection with Charles E. Curran, a professor of moral theology at The Catholic University. I esteemed him as a close personal friend and regarded him as more moderate than than many of his colleagues in the field of moral theology. In the classroom he had a reputation for insisting that his students study carefully the official teaching of the Church, even on points where he personally dissented from it. But he was also very outspoken and given to organizing opposition to the hierarchical teaching when he found himself in disagreement.

Curran had been a primary mover in orchestrating the dissent from *Humanae vitae* in 1968, and had in no way modified his positions. After a long exchange of letters with him, beginning even before Joseph Ratzinger's tenure as Prefect, the Congregation for the Doctrine of the Faith published a letter declaring that Curran was "neither suitable nor eligible" to teach as a Catholic theologian. Cardinal James Hickey, as Chancellor of The Catholic University, had no choice but to withdraw Curran's canonical mission, which he was probably anxious to do in any case. This action resulted in a long judicial process within The Catholic University and later in a court case.

In serving on the committee of the faculty senate appointed to deal with the case, I supported its findings to the effect that the Chancellor's withdrawal of the canonical mission was justified and that Father Curran could not continue to teach in the theology department without a canonical mission. The committee also judged that in view of Curran's position as a tenured faculty member, the university should offer him a teaching position in a department, such as those of religion or sociology, in which a canonical mission was not required. The trustees of the university did in fact offer Father Curran an appointment in the sociology department, but no agreement could be reached on the precise conditions under which he would teach. He then instituted an unsuccessful civil suit against the university and the archbishop. Father Curran later moved on to other universities, eventually settling at Southern Methodist University in Dallas. My own view is that he is an intelligent and forceful thinker and a committed Catholic priest. But it is probably better for him not to be teaching in a situation that requires a canonical mission, which gives the theologian a quasi-magisterial platform in the Church.

My principal theological publication during my years at The Catholic University was probably *Models of Revelation,* published in 1983.[8] On the whole the method in this work was similar to that used in *Models of the Church.* For the earlier history of the treatise, I simply presupposed what I had written in an earlier work, *Revelation Theology: A History.*[9] After setting forth five models in current theology, and analyzing their strengths and weaknesses, I proceeded to develop my personal positions by using the concept of "symbolic communication" as a dialectical tool. I pointed out that although symbol plays a role in all the models, the concept of symbol differs from one model to the next. I argued in favor of symbolic realism, and rejected the predominantly subjectivist notion of symbol current in what George Lindbeck describes as the "experiential-expressivist" school of thought. I therefore found myself able to affirm the predominantly symbolic character of revelation without minimizing the historical and doctrinal aspects that were so

8. Avery Dulles, *Models of Revelation* (Garden City: Doubleday, 1983). This volume has been reprinted with a new preface by Orbis Books, Maryknoll, New York, in 1992.

9. Avery Dulles, *Revelation Theology: A History* (New York: Herder and Herder, 1969).

prominent in Catholic teaching. Those who maintain a subjectivist view of symbol have difficulty maintaining solidarity with the Catholic tradition.

In my *Models of Revelation,* as elsewhere, I have been reserved in drawing on contemporary experience as a distinct theological source. Experience is a very ambiguous thing, shaped by the presuppositions and categories that one brings to it. It can be a theological source, but only if the experience itself is informed by the gospel. One of the most persistent temptations of theology is excessive accommodation to the tastes and fashions of the day. In addressing the present-day situation, theology should take advantage of whatever points of insertion can be found for the Christian message but it must also be prepared to challenge the prevalent mentality.

In taking a somewhat critical attitude toward the dominant secular culture I have been influenced by the Ignatian principle of acting against whatever can lead one away from total faithfulness to Christ and the hierarchical Church (the justly celebrated *"agere contra"* of the Spiritual Exercises). St. Ignatius made it a rule to do the direct opposite of what a worldly or heretical spirit inclines one to do. The early Jesuits may have carried this principle too far in rejecting everything that savored of Protestantism, but the contemporary trend among theologians is, I think, to be too accommodating. Catholics are under enormous pressure from the media and from secular academia to conform to the spirit of the times.

Toward the end of my stay at The Catholic University I published *The Catholicity of the Church,* the Martin C. D'Arcy Lectures I had delivered at Oxford in 1983.[10] The book is in many ways a complement to my *Models of the Church,* more expressive of my own ecclesiology. I surveyed the various dimensions of catholicity and sought to show how they come together in Catholic Christianity. The structures of Catholicism, I contended, are providentially instituted to promote and safeguard the catholicity of the Church and of the Christian faith. Without these structures neither the purity nor the fullness of Christianity could be assured.

VI. Return to Fordham

In 1988, having reached the statutory retirement age, I completed my service on the faculty of The Catholic University and accepted an invitation to hold a university chair at Fordham, where I had begun my teaching career 37 years earlier. This chair required several public lectures each year and involved some limited teaching responsibilities, but at the same time gave me sufficient freedom to accept a variety of visiting appointments and outside speaking engagements, and to serve on a number of national and international committees.

---

10. Avery Dulles, *The Catholicity of the Church* (Oxford: Clarendon, 1985). The paperback edition, first issued in 1987, has since been reprinted.

After moving to Fordham I was able to write a book on faith that I had long been contemplating. Drawing on the descriptive definition of faith given in the Letter to the Hebrews (11:1), I chose as my title *The Assurance of Things Hoped For.*[11] My principal purpose in this work was to redirect attention to the classical questions that were currently neglected and to show the abiding value of the great authors of the past who had profoundly investigated the nature and attributes of faith. For the most part I adhered to the doctrine of Thomas Aquinas in the *Summa theologiae,* but I introduced a few modifications to bring that doctrine into line with the more biblical and ecumenical approach of Vatican II. In view of the richness of the biblical and theological tradition concerning faith, I found it possible to reduce my own contribution almost to the vanishing point. If there is any originality in the book, it consists in the selection of what I regard as the high points of the tradition, and the avoidance of byroads that in many cases have proved to be blind alleys. It was my intention to indicate that not all recent innovations deserve to be hailed as positive contributions. Whereas modern authors usually strain to give the impression that they are saying something new, it might not be a bad idea to imitate the medieval writers, who generally tried to hide any signs of originality and to adhere as

---

11. Avery Dulles, *The Assurance of Things Hoped For: A Theology of Christian Faith* (New York: Oxford University Press, 1994).

closely as possible to the views of esteemed prede-
cessors, especially the Church Fathers.

Almost simultaneously with my book of faith
I published in two editions *The Craft of Theology*,
a collection of essays on theological method.[12]
Whereas authors such as Bernard Lonergan had
tried to construct a methodology that would be
independent of the theology of revelation and ecclesiology, I deliberately took a different line. My
objective was to show how the conclusions of my
theology of revelation and of Church could serve
to ground a theological method that was loyally
Catholic and at the same time open to development. I consistently referred to the Church as
the living community within which the theologian
works and to which the theologian's conclusions
must be submitted. I pointed out the reciprocal
relations between theology and the ecclesiastical
magisterium, and the value of the magisterium
for reliably articulating the beliefs that the theologian must seek to understand.

VII. The Present Situation

The quantity of theological publication in the past
twenty years has increased exponentially. University theology departments have professors of
greater academic competence than has been the
case within recent memory. Sophisticated new
methods of literary criticism, ideology criticism,

---

12. Avery Dulles, *The Craft of Theology: From Symbol to System*
(New York: Crossroad, 1992). An expanded edition with two
new chapters was published in paperback, 1995.

structuralism, and depth psychology are being applied to the Scriptures and other authoritative texts. In spite of these achievements, however, it is difficult to say that Christian theology is in a very healthy condition. Not infrequently one hears laments that the giants of earlier generations seem to have died without leaving comparable successors. Reflecting on this situation, I am inclined to believe that the crisis of theology reflects a crisis of faith that is deeply rooted in the modern spirit.

This crisis is manifest in the conflict of interpretations of Vatican II. In the first decade after the Council, extending roughly to 1975, the dominant trend was to stress the novelty of the Council and to treat its reaffirmations of earlier Church teachings as mere concessions to a minority of conservative bishops who lacked the true spirit of Vatican II. Following the logic of this hermeneutic, many commentators felt impelled to go beyond the Council, to reject its compromises, and to work for a Church that is more modern, more democratic, more open to change.

I have been increasingly conscious of the inadequacies of this interpretation. Although Vatican II did speak with accents that were genuinely new, the Council Fathers were very serious in wishing to stand in continuity with the teaching of earlier popes and councils. In union with the whole Catholic tradition they were convinced that the Church was a visible society, divinely founded, and subsisting in the Roman Catholic communion of the present day. They maintained that the popes and bishops could teach with the authority of Christ, govern as Christ's representatives, and celebrate the sacraments as participants in his priestly office. The Catholic Church, according to Vatican II, was a "necessary" society in the sense that all are bound to adhere to its teaching, to join it, and remain within it as members. Only inculpable ignorance can excuse one from these obligations. All of these traditional affirmations were seen by the Council Fathers – rightly, I believe – as matters of faith.

These central teachings of Vatican II are widely contested or ignored. In countries such as our own it is not difficult to encounter Catholics who, perhaps under the influence of secular models of society, speak of the Church as if it were a humanly instituted community that could change its teaching, its sacramental worship, and its forms of government at will. These Catholics regard the Church not as necessary society but rather as a voluntary association of individuals who share a common project. In some circles one finds a species of Catholic congregationalism, in which it is assumed that any group of worshipers would have the right to authorize some of its own members to celebrate the liturgy. This congregationalism is combined with a kind of religious consumerism, according to which local churches would be entitled to modify doctrines and liturgical texts to suit the current state of public opinion and the tastes of the worshipers. Instead of being bound to conform themselves to the teaching and discipline of the Church, individuals would be morally free to opt out of the Church if it ceased to respond to their wishes and reflect their views.

Catholics who adhere to the teachings of the Councils, including Trent, Vatican I, and Vatican II, tend to be characterized as traditionalists or conservatives, and in some cases merit the label. Every Christian should be a conservative in the sense of wishing to safeguard the truth revealed by God in Jesus Christ, and entrusted to the Church as its authorized custodian. Conservativism, however, can turn into an ideology when it ceases to be open to pastoral adaptations and becomes defensive and polemical. Too often the advocates of conservatism are content to form a party in the Church, engaging in divisive tactics. Some traditionalists in their anger misrepresent their adversaries, impugn the conduct of bishops and popes, and silently or overtly reject the teaching of Vatican II on issues such as religious freedom, ecumenism, and dialogue. An extreme exemplification of this anti-Modernism would be the late Archbishop Marcel Lefebvre.

Although moderate Catholics strive to be receptive to both the old and the new in Vatican II, the conflict between the liberal and conservative wings has markedly politicized the Church. Both sides are tempted to subordinate an even-handed concern for truth to the demands of a party spirit in which every action and statement is evaluated according to whether it supports one cause or the other. The Church as a universal communion is severely wounded by such partisanship. Members of the two factions tend to publish in different journals, to join different professional societies, and to patronize different educational institutions. The opposed parties seek to discredit their opponents, often by acrimonious attacks that are uncharitable and even unjust.

In this polarized situation it becomes increasingly difficult to settle doctrinal questions through any kind of rational discourse. Commonly accepted criteria are hard to come by. Before the Council, it would have been easy to resolve many doctrinal disputes by appealing to the clear teaching of Scripture, the creeds, the teaching of popes and councils, and the consensus of theologians. But in the circles I am here describing, the authoritative sources are permitted to speak only to the extent that they can be interpreted as supporting one's own cause. Hermeneutics degenerates into the art of twisting texts to make them mean what one wants them to say. If the texts cannot be so interpreted, sociocritical analysis is applied to undermine their authority. Even the most sacred sources are frequently contested, not only by reforming Catholics but in some cases also by traditionalists. The diminished respect for ecclesiastical authority makes it difficult for the hierarchical teachers to make binding decisions. Theologians are not in a better position to promote concord. Lacking common goals, a common methodology, and a common language, theology finds its status as a discipline thrown into question. Lacking clear principles, it runs the risk of degenerating into journalism or propaganda.

The progressive party in the Catholic Church today falls into many of the exaggerations that I have described in my original text under the rubric of liberalism. In several dense paragraphs I alluded to the individualism, majoritarianism, progressivism, relativism, pragmatism, and metaphysical agnosticism inherent in the liberal project. At the time these tendencies were external to the Catholic Church, but today they have penetrated deep into the ranks of the Catholic faithful, including segments of the theological community.

The last of these tendencies, metaphysical agnosticism, is in some ways the most fundamental. Immanuel Kant maintained that nothing speculatively true and certain can be said about God and other immaterial realities, because the proper domain of the human mind is limited to phenomena that come through the senses. Accepting this agnosticism, many of our contemporaries discard the classical doctrine of analogy and speak as though all statements about God were mere metaphors. They tend to blur the distinction between attributes such as "good," "wise," and "loving," which are literally though analogously predicated of God, and metaphorical statements, such as calling God a fortress, a rock, or a shield. Carried to an extreme, agnosticism dissolves the very idea of God into a symbol or metaphor for something else, which cannot be directly known. This procedure strikes at the heart of the whole Christian enterprise, since no one can pray to a metaphor or worship a symbol manufactured by the human mind.

In the politicized atmosphere of our time, some theologians frame their speech about God on grounds of practical expediency. For example, some like to call God compassionate and vulnerable, but they discountenance terms such as "eternal," "sovereign," and "omniscient" because these concepts underline the inferiority of the human condition. Even speech about God as Father, Son, and Holy Spirit, though authorized by Sacred Scripture and the unbroken tradition of many centuries, is being called into question because it seems to have social consequences that some find unacceptable. The criterion of consequentialism assumes priority over that of speculative truth.

The realism of Christian faith is no longer taken for granted, even by professed believers. In much of the current theological literature faith is exalted only because of its supposed value in bringing about mental health and social progress. It is said to give peace of mind, psychological balance, or a laudable concern for the oppressed. We have gone a long way from the biblical authors, who maintained that faith in the true God was important because no one but the true God could impart salvation. For them it was essential to place one's trust in the One who can be trusted. In this respect sound theology supports the biblical authors. Strictly speaking, salvation is not an achievement of faith but a gift of God.

In spite of the agitation from both extremes, the Catholic Church remains a communion of tradition and authority, open to dialogue and progress. Thanks to its deposit of faith, it has the resources to cope with the modern crisis of truth. It adheres to the truth not only through abstract intellectual knowledge but through intimate experience of God, who makes himself present in the Church's life of prayer and worship. The Church is held to Christ by the Spirit of truth that has been conferred upon it and by tasting Christ's presence in the sacraments.

During my years as a Catholic I have grown in my confidence in the "charism of truth" conferred upon the hierarchical leadership. Because of its firm hierarchical structures the Church does not yield easily to quasi-political pressures. Pope John Paul II, who understands and encourages democratic institutions in secular society, shows no doubt in his own mind that the Church is a hierarchical society, in which the responsible leadership lies inalienably with the pope and the bishops, who have received their office by apostolic succession. Like earlier popes, he has used his office in creative ways, adapted to the contemporary world situation. Cardinal Ratzinger, one of the ablest living theologians, has shown firmness and moderation in exercising his role of vigilance as prefect of the Congregation for the Doctrine of the Faith. By and large, the bishops continue to defend Catholic orthodoxy, so that the unity of the Church and heritage of faith are not in peril.

In 1975, celebrating the tenth anniversary of the close of Vatican II, Pope Paul VI summarized the main objective of the Council as that of enabling the Church to proclaim the gospel more effectively to the people of the twentieth century. With his apostolic exhortation *On Evangelization in the Modern World* Paul VI launched a new era of evangelization, which Pope John Paul II has strongly reaffirmed. The popes are acutely conscious of the growing confusion and darkness, the deterioration of moral standards, and the descent of millions into an abyss of dehumanizing poverty. They are convinced that the gospel of Christ is needed to restore a sense of human dignity and a respect for the moral law. The gospel, as they depict it, has not been given only to Christians, and still less only to people of the Western hemisphere. As a leaven, the gospel extends its salutary influence far beyond the visible limits of the Church. God wants all men and women to come to the knowledge of Christ, the one mediator of salvation; he intends human society to be rebuilt in the light of Christ, who points the way to what Paul VI memorably called a "civilization of love."

Will the call to the new evangelization be heard? The answer depends to no small extent on the future development of theology. The faith cannot be confidently preached unless it is firmly believed. It cannot be firmly believed unless Christians regain their sense that God has really revealed himself, and that biblical teaching, as interpreted in the tradition, embodies the truth of revelation. To the extent that Catholics fall prey to modern tendencies such as metaphysical agnosticism (and consequent aberrations such as pragmatism, historical relativism, dogmatic pluralism, and the allergy to authority) they cannot hope to be carriers of the gospel.

Many Catholic theologians, unclear about the importance of the faith that comes through hearing, have been reluctant to align themselves with the call to proclaim the gospel. Conservative Protestant groups, although they have a conception of the gospel that I would regard as very inadequate, are far more committed to the task of evangelization. Having drifted away from the missionary commitments of their forebears, Catholics are only beginning to catch up with Pentecostal and biblicist Protestants. Yet the Catholic Church, with its rich intellectual and cultural heritage, has resources for evangelization that are available to no other group. We need a more outgoing, dynamic Church, less distracted by internal controversy, more focused on the Lordship of Jesus Christ, more responsive to the Spirit, and more capable of united action.

Thanks in great part to the doctrinal firmness of the Holy See, the flow of converts to the Catholic

Church, which slowed down to a small trickle during the confusion after Vatican II, has resumed in recent years. Many Protestants and Anglicans, especially those in the mainstream churches, sense that their own communions are falling prey to current secular ideologies and that the heritage of faith is being eroded. They still find in the Catholic Church a steadfast commitment to the basic truths of Christianity, including the doctrines of the Trinity, the divinity of Christ, the resurrection, and the sole mediatorship of Christ. They are attracted by the strong sacramental life of Catholicism and by its unity throughout space and time. The motives of those joining the Catholic Church in the 1990s are strikingly similar to my own motives in 1940. Some of them, however, consider that the term "convert" does not apply to them, since they experience Catholicism as the fulfillment of the faith that they professed in the community to which they previously belonged. In my own case "convert" was the right term, because I experienced a radical change of perspective in coming to the Catholic faith. For me it was a passage from darkness into light.

Catholics with roots in other traditions, Christian or non-Christian, having experienced the joy of coming to the fullness of truth, frequently have greater motivation than others to engage in evangelization. They may have a special vocation to remind Catholics who have been raised in the faith of the features that make the

Church attractive to outsiders. They may appropriately warn Catholics against imitating the mistakes that have occasioned the decline of mainstream Protestantism. Although Protestantism is a very complex phenomenon, admirable in certain aspects, many continue to experience it in the diluted form that I have described in the first part of this book.

VIII. A Final Word

The original work to which I append these reflections bears the title, *A Testimonial to Grace*. I meant that title as an expression of thanks to God for the ways in which he had led me. As I look over the course of my life, it seems everything in it has been providential. What would my life have been if I had not spent some years in Europe as a boy, if I had followed my family tradition in going to Princeton rather than Harvard, if the Second World War had not interrupted my studies at law school? No one can answer questions such as these. But I can say that through the tangled web of events, I was constantly being led to fulfill my deepest aspirations and what I dare to regard as my vocation.

Even as a Jesuit I have not planned my own ways. I studied where I was told to, taking the prescribed courses and never making any special requests on my own behalf. I taught philosophy in my years of regency because I was assigned to do so, and at the time I fully expected to be sent to do doctoral studies in that field. But while

I was studying theology, I was unexpectedly directed to make that my specialty, thus fulfilling what had been my unexpressed desire. In my studies and early teaching career I was greatly helped by the guidance of Jesuit theologians such as John Courtney Murray and Gustave Weigel, two of the giants of their day.

Throughout my teaching career I have had assignments of great interest to me. The fields of revelation, faith, ecclesiology, and ecumenism have never ceased to fascinate me. I have been privileged to teach in a great variety of institutions, Catholic and non-Catholic, and to profit from cordial ecumenical contacts. As a Jesuit I have profited from association with colleagues all over the world. When traveling in Latin America, Europe, Africa, and the Far East I have been welcomed by fellow priests, by religious, and especially by Jesuits as a friend and brother. If I had been asked to choose the course of my life I would not have done as well as the leading of Providence and the direction of superiors have done for me. I can honestly say that there is no one in the world whom I have cause to envy. All of this is not of my own deserving. It is God's gift, and he alone deserves the praise.

I am conscious, of course, of my limitations. In some respects I fall below the standards of pastoral performance that should be expected of an ordinary priest. I admire from afar the achievements of great confessors, preachers, mystics, missionaries, penitents, and martyrs, who no doubt do far more for God's glory than an entire host of theologians. But I have received a different vocation, more suited to my capabilities and inclinations.

Even in theology, which has been my special field of concern, I make no claim to be a major figure. I cannot aspire to the speculative brilliance of a Rahner or a Lonergan, or the erudition of a de Lubac, a von Balthasar, or a Congar. But I rejoice at having been able to read the works of these great leaders, and to have known each of them personally. Together with the great thinkers of the past, they have helped me to attain a wisdom far beyond what I could have achieved by my own powers.

When I entered the Catholic Church I made a venture that appeared foolhardy in the eyes of most of my family and friends. As a vowed religious, I took up a career that would make no sense unless the Catholic faith were true. If the Kingdom is the pearl of great price, the treasure buried in the field, one should be prepared to give up everything else to acquire it. It has always seemed to me that if God is God, his honor and glory must be the first priority. Although I cannot rival the generous dedication of Sts. Paul and Ignatius of Loyola, I am, like them, content to be employed in the service of Christ and the gospel, whether in sickness or in health, in good repute or ill repute. I am immeasurably grateful for the years in which the Lord has permitted me to serve him in a society that bears as its motto: *Ad majorem*

Dei gloriam. I trust that his grace will not fail me, and that I will not fail his grace, in the years to come.